GW00357616

The ITIL® Guide to Software and IT Asset Management

London: TSO

part of Williams Lea Tag

Published by TSO (The Stationery Office), part of Williams Lea
Tag, and available from:

Online
www.tsoshop.co.uk

Mail, Telephone, Fax & E-mail
TSO
PO Box 29, Norwich, NR3 1GN
Telephone orders/General enquiries: 0333 202 5070
Fax orders: 0333 202 5080
E-mail: customer.services@tso.co.uk
Textphone 0333 202 5077

TSO@Blackwell and other Accredited Agents

The information contained in this publication is believed to be correct at the time of manufacture. Whilst care has been taken to ensure that the information is accurate, the publisher can accept no responsibility for any errors or omissions or for changes to the details given.

AXELOS, the AXELOS logo, the AXELOS swirl logo, ITIL®, MoP®, M_o_R®, MoV®, MSP®, P3M3®, P3O®, PRINCE2® and PRINCE2 Agile® are registered trade marks of AXELOS Limited.

RESILIA™ and the Best Management Practice Official Publisher logo are trade marks of AXELOS Limited.

A CIP catalogue record for this book is available from the British Library.

A Library of Congress CIP catalogue record has been applied for.

First edition The Stationery Office copyright 2009
Second edition The Stationery Office copyright 2018

ISBN 9780113315482

Printed in the United Kingdom by The Stationery Office
P002901797   c3   01/18

Contents

List of figures and tables

Preface

The ITIL® publication, *Software Asset Management* (known as the ITIL SAM guide), was published in 2003 by The Stationery Office for the Office of Government Commerce, and was part of the ITIL v2 series of books. With the publication of ITIL v3 in 2007, the need arose for an update to reflect the changes in ITIL, and in 2009 *ITIL v3 Guide to Software Asset Management* was published. In 2011, ITIL was updated again; this time the ITIL framework was referred to as ITIL 2011.

This second edition of the 2009 guide is the first major revision of all previous content, and explicitly covers both software asset management (SAM) and the more inclusive IT asset management (ITAM). Much has changed in the areas of SAM and ITAM since 2003, as discussed in Chapter 4, and there is now also far more expertise in these disciplines. This revision has drawn on the shared knowledge of a large number of experts within the profession.

This edition also brings a change of focus, which is now on the IT service management (ITSM) practitioner who wants to implement best practice in SAM/ITAM. This edition is still usable by the non-ITSM practitioner, but ITIL background information is not provided. Non-ITSM practitioners are strongly encouraged to take ITIL training, at least to the foundation level.

Revising this guide has been an exhilarating experience, resulting in new knowledge and insights for the authors and reviewers alike. As the profession continues to develop, we must also continue to learn and to share; therefore we welcome comments on this guide for future updates.

The noted surgeon and writer Atul Gawande (2014) made the following observations about the medical profession which are equally relevant to SAM/ITAM:

> 'The volume of knowledge and skill has exceeded our individual capabilities.'

> '… even the most experienced people, even the most expert fail, and … we need the humility to be able to understand that.'

We would do well to remember his words.

Colin Rudd
colin.rudd@itemsltd.com

David Bicket
david.bicket@m-assure.com

October 2017

Foreword

Since AXELOS published *ITIL Practitioner Guidance* in 2016, we have seen a significant adoption of the guiding principles whenever ITIL and ITSM are discussed. The first of these principles is 'Focus on value'. This publication helps organizations to better leverage their software and other IT assets in order to improve the value delivered to customers. It describes how IT assets (as things with potential value) can be better mapped to the value realized, and how ITAM helps with this by including the actual value gained from costs savings, risk management, licence compliance and enhanced security.

This value-focused holistic view aligns well with the current thinking in ITIL. Using the well-integrated examples throughout this publication, ITSM professionals will be able to link the guidance to their own daily work. I believe that ITSM professionals who use ITIL for improving the ITSM capabilities in their own organizations or for their customers will find this guide an invaluable resource to better understand SAM and ITAM, and to put what they have learned into practice.

Kaimar Karu

Former Head of Product Strategy and Development, AXELOS

About AXELOS

AXELOS is a joint venture company co-owned by the UK Government's Cabinet Office and Capita plc. It is responsible for developing, enhancing and promoting a number of best-practice methodologies used globally by professionals working primarily in project, programme and portfolio management, IT service management and cyber resilience.

The methodologies, including ITIL®, PRINCE2®, MSP® and the new collection of cyber resilience best-practice products, RESILIA™, are adopted in more than 150 countries to improve employees' skills, knowledge and competence in order to make both individuals and organizations work more effectively.

In addition to globally recognized qualifications, AXELOS equips professionals with a wide range of content, templates and toolkits through its membership scheme, its professional development programme and its online community of practitioners and experts.

Visit www.axelos.com for the latest news about how AXELOS is making organizations more effective and registration details to join the AXELOS online community. If you have specific queries or requests, or would like to be added to the AXELOS mailing list, please contact ask@axelos.com.

PUBLICATIONS

AXELOS publishes a comprehensive range of guidance, including:

- *ITIL® Service Strategy*
- *ITIL® Service Design*
- *ITIL® Service Transition*
- *ITIL® Service Operation*
- *ITIL® Continual Service Improvement*
- *ITIL® Practitioner Guidance*
- *PRINCE2 Agile®*
- *Managing Successful Projects with PRINCE2®*
- *Directing Successful Projects with PRINCE2®*
- *Management of Portfolios (MoP®)*
- *Managing Successful Programmes (MSP®)*
- *Management of Risk: Guidance for Practitioners (M_o_R®)*
- *Portfolio, Programme and Project Offices (P3O®)*
- Portfolio, Programme and Project Management Maturity Model (P3M3®)
- *Management of Value (MoV®)*
- *RESILIA™: Cyber Resilience Best Practice.*

Full details of the range of materials published under the AXELOS Global Best Practice banner, including *The ITIL® Guide to Software and IT Asset Management*, can be found at:

https://www.axelos.com/best-practice-solutions

If you would like to inform AXELOS of any changes that may be required to *The ITIL® Guide to Software and IT Asset Management* or any other AXELOS publication, please log them at:

https://www.axelos.com/best-practice-feedback

CONTACT INFORMATION

Full details on how to contact AXELOS can be found at:

https://www.axelos.com

For further information on qualifications and training accreditation, please visit:

https://www.axelos.com/certifications

https://www.axelos.com/becoming-an-axelos-partner

For all other enquiries, please email:

ask@axelos.com

Acknowledgements

COLIN RUDD

Colin has worked in the IT industry for more than 50 years, during which time he has held many different positions and roles. Earlier in his career he specialized in the design, development, implementation and management of networks, including the Moscow Olympics network and some of the early B2B and electronic data interchange networks (such as Tradanet®). He has written numerous books on infrastructure and ITSM, and was involved in the development and authoring of every version of ITIL.

Recognized worldwide as a leader in the implementation of infrastructure and ITSM practices, Colin speaks internationally on these topics. He has mentored and coached many senior IT executives and management teams in the development of their skills and their people, and has thus been instrumental in the implementation of numerous IT management systems.

Colin has been involved in the development of the international standards ISO 20000 (service management) and ISO 19770 (software asset management) as well as helping to establish the ISO 20000 certification and qualification schemes. His contributions to the IT and ITSM industries were recognized in 2002 when the IT Service Management Forum presented him with its lifetime achievement award.

DAVID BICKET

David has worked in IT for 47 years and been active in software asset management (SAM) and IT asset management (ITAM) for almost half his career. He project-managed and contributed extensively to the original ITIL guide, *Software Asset Management* (2003), and from 2007 to 2014 was the convener of the ISO working group responsible for SAM and ITAM standards (ISO/IEC JTC1 SC7 WG21). He was also a co-editor of the recent revision of the ITAM standard 19770-1.

David's career of more than 20 years with several major accounting firms around the world culminated as a director for Deloitte. His work for major software publishers included audits of IT resellers, partners and users. Earlier he held IT-related positions within the banking, IT and chemical industries and in governmental IT audit. He has been a qualified accountant (CPA), information systems auditor (CISA) and banker (ACIB).

David has also been extensively involved in other areas: developing assurance programmes for cloud service providers; drawing up model terms and conditions for cloud computing contracts; and working on personal data protection issues. He currently has his own company m-Assure Ltd (www.m-assure.com).

REVIEWERS

The following have all contributed to the content contained within this publication, either directly, by reviewing, or both:

Peter Beruk, ITAM Consulting Group; Ron Brill, Anglepoint; Rory Canavan, SAM Charter; Blake Gollnick, SHI; Peter Hubbard, Pink Elephant; Steve Klos, TagVault; Jan Minartz, Deloitte; Harry Repo, CBO Consulting; Johannes Schmidt, KPMG; Martin Thompson, ITAM Review; Diederik Van Der Sijpe, Deloitte; Matt Ward, SoftCat.

We have not repeated the names of the contributors to either the original 2003 edition or the 2009 update because the current edition has been so extensively revised. However, those earlier works, and their contributors, laid the foundation for this present work.

PUBLISHER'S ACKNOWLEDGEMENTS

The publisher would like to give special thanks to the following experts who thoroughly reviewed the manuscript and returned timely valuable feedback:

Kylie Fowler, ITAM Intelligence; David Foxen, independent consultant; Jennette King, independent consultant.

How to use this guide

This guide should be of interest to anybody involved in the acquisition, development, operation, use and retirement of IT assets within an organization. It should be of particular interest to ITSM practitioners who wish to focus on software and IT asset management, most notably these three types of individual:

■ directors and other members of senior management with corporate governance responsibility, including responsibility for IT assets and the risks associated with them. These individuals will find Chapters 1, 4 and 8 the most pertinent.

■ ITSM practitioners assuming responsibility for managing, investigating, implementing or improving asset management processes or asset management systems. These individuals will be interested in the entire guide, starting with Chapters 1 and 2.

■ non-ITSM practitioners assuming similar responsibilities. These individuals will be interested in the entire guide, but they are also strongly encouraged to take ITIL training to at least the foundation level.

Chapters 1–15 cover topics from which a SAM/ITAM practitioner should benefit in the discharge of their normal responsibilities. The appendices provide further detailed information for specific topics.

The main part of this guide is organized as indicated in Figure 0.1. Everything operates within an external context, as discussed in Chapters 2–5. Internal drivers are covered in Chapters 6 and 7. The five 'Ps' are discussed as follows:

■ **People** The people involved in ITAM, their roles and responsibilities (Chapter 8)
■ **Policy** Approaches to specifying policy (Chapter 9)
■ **Processes** The management processes required for effective ITAM (Chapter 10)
■ **Products** The management technology and tools used within the ITAM processes (Chapter 11)
■ **Partners** External organizations involved within ITAM processes, including publishers, resellers and ITAM consultants (Chapter 12).

There are three chapters on the separate topics of implementation (Chapter 13), security (Chapter 14) and licence compliance audits (Chapter 15).

The appendices cover:

■ **Software** Overviews of the software distribution channels and licensing
■ **ISO ITAM standard** Overview of the standard
■ **Technology** Considerations in selecting SAM/ITAM tools; a discussion of technological enablers (the ISO information structure standards); and possible ITAM database contents
■ **Partners** Guidance on partner contracting, and a checklist to help in selecting SAM/ITAM partners.

Additional guidance and reference documents are available which should be consulted as appropriate (see Further information). These include the ITIL publications (in particular the five core ITIL publications), *ITIL Practitioner Guidance* (2016), and the ITIL Glossary and Abbreviations.

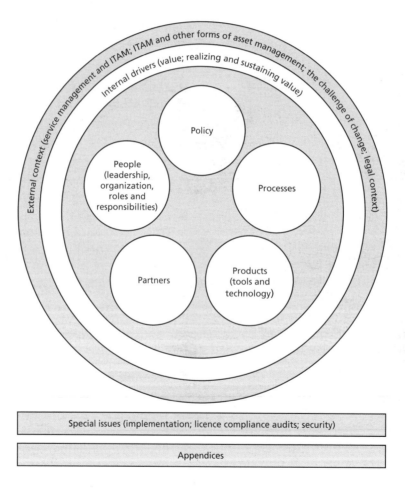

Figure 0.1 Structure of the ITIL SAM/ITAM guide

Introduction 1

1 Introduction

1.1 WHY INCLUDE SAM AND ITAM IN ITIL?

IT service management (ITSM) is a powerful discipline, and ITIL is the best known and most widely used best-practice framework for ITSM. With such a powerful framework, why is there a need to provide ITSM practitioners with specific guidance for SAM and ITAM?

The reason is that SAM and ITAM address management needs in IT that are closely linked to ITSM (and without which ITSM as a whole cannot successfully function), but which are not the primary focus. Licence management is one of the most obvious examples where best practice is needed but not provided by the core ITSM methodology of ITIL. The ITSM practitioner (and the practitioner's organization) therefore benefits if good SAM/ITAM practice can be implemented in support of ITSM in an integrated way. Chapter 2 covers this relationship in more detail.

The first guiding principle of ITIL is 'Focus on value', and good ITAM delivers significant value. Chapter 6 covers the many types of value that good ITAM can deliver, including cost savings, risk management, licence compliance, enhanced security and improved overall management. Chapter 7 covers the factors which facilitate or inhibit success in ITAM and those that enable value to be sustained in the longer term.

1.2 WHY REVISE THE EXISTING ITIL SAM GUIDE?

When the ITIL SAM guide was first published in 2003, the term 'software asset management' was already in limited use but with many alternative definitions and associated frameworks. The ITIL SAM guide provided what has subsequently become the most-used definition and helped drive common understandings and approaches to the area.

Both SAM and ITAM are now well-established, but unfortunately a wide gulf has developed between what is included in these two disciplines, what senior management understands by the terms, and what is covered by the job roles that are typically called SAM and ITAM. This revision is intended to help bridge those gaps and to help everyone understand the disciplines, regardless of their professional perspective.

The left side of Figure 1.1 illustrates the respective scopes of SAM and ITAM in principle, according to the definitions given in section 1.3. Textbook definitions, however, seldom correspond with senior management's understanding regarding these disciplines and roles. The top right of Figure 1.1 illustrates how SAM is often perceived as being only about licence compliance.

This management perception is both a blessing and a curse. Positively, it can lead to the provision of funding and support when there are major licence compliance issues which can be addressed by SAM. (Note that choosing to implement SAM is only one of the possible reactions to licence compliance issues; see Chapter 15.) However, senior management perceptions can also create constraints if a SAM implementation is driven solely by licence compliance. SAM, when properly implemented, is typically involved with more than this; for example,

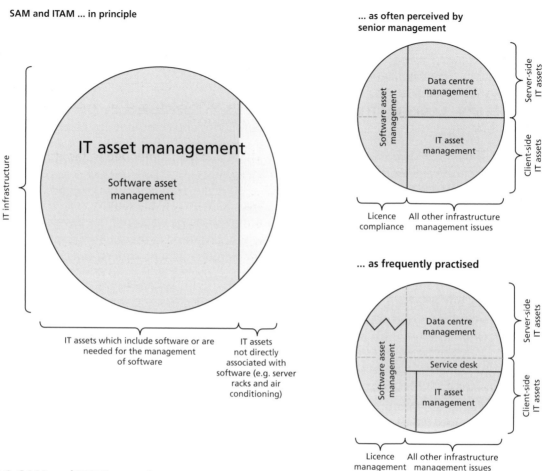

Figure 1.1 SAM and ITAM overview

it increasingly focuses on practices which can save the organization considerable money, such as licence harvesting (see section 6.2) and recycling.

The bottom right of Figure 1.1 illustrates fairly common scopes for SAM and ITAM as actually practised.

The two diagrams on the right side of Figure 1.1 demonstrate another significant observation: the frequent split between server-side and client-side IT asset management. Together these two areas constitute full IT infrastructure management. However, the server side often does not think of its role as being IT asset management, but rather as infrastructure management. The server side is only part of the whole, and it is the part which is more impacted by the move to the cloud. Also, in some organizations there is a three-way split with networks managing their assets separately from both client and server sides. This situation creates even more issues with SAM/ITAM practices.

Server-side ITAM is still ITAM. The only question is one of labelling. Some practitioners of server-side ITAM insist, correctly, that they are doing ITAM, including server-side licence compliance. This guide strongly supports that usage but also recognizes that in practice the term is more often used to describe client-side asset management.

Another of the factors which tends to separate server-side from client-side practitioners is the complexity of some server-side technologies (e.g. server virtualization, clustering, data centres and networks). Both the technical and licensing expertise needed to deal with this complexity is challenging to develop and maintain.

These differences between theory, perception and practice sometimes result in conflicts between SAM/ITAM practitioners and their management when the practitioners try to practise more of their discipline than is covered by management perceptions. Furthermore, SAM programmes are often shut down after running for only a few years because a narrowly defined licence compliance role is no longer seen as a priority after the initial savings ('low-hanging fruit') from them have been obtained, and there is only limited scope for further savings of this type (for guidance on sustainability, see section 7.7).

This guide covers the full spectrum of the SAM and ITAM disciplines, which not only includes but also exceeds the more limited understanding and practice of those terms. In doing so, it seeks to support a more inclusive view of these disciplines and to help extend the roles labelled SAM and ITAM to match the new challenges of IT, break down 'silos' where they hinder proper IT asset management, thereby benefiting both organizations and practitioners.

Key message

Good SAM and ITAM, not constrained to just licence compliance but serving all of IT and the entire organization, will facilitate the work of many other units, such as IT security and the IT service desk.

This guide is also intended to facilitate better integration of SAM and ITAM with ITSM. The original ITIL SAM guide was aligned with ITIL v2, but this edition has been extensively revised to align with current ITIL guidance. (Throughout this guide, 'ITIL' is used to refer to the ITIL 2011 core publications on ITSM, unless otherwise specified.)

This guidance can be tailored to fit any organization, regardless of size and of whether it is already committed to ITIL best-practice approaches in all areas or intending to adopt such guidance on a more limited basis. If this is the first ITIL guide to be used within an organization, we strongly recommend that relevant staff familiarize themselves with the full range of guidance available from ITIL (see www.axelos.com/best-practice-solutions/itil and the related user group website at www.itsmfi.org; also Chapter 2).

This guide is intended to be publisher- and platform-neutral and to provide impartial, practical advice. Specific products are not mentioned. Most of the coverage is as applicable to PC workstations and smartphones as to servers and mainframes, and to network communications equipment and cloud-based services.

Key recommendations for senior management

To start your ITAM initiative

■ **Vision** Determine why ITAM is needed in a way that aligns with the overall organizational vision and objectives. Ideally the vision should include other ITIL service areas and be aligned with other business and organizational strategies and visions (see section 7.1.1).

■ **Initial responsibility and accountability** Allocate (to a member of staff with adequate authority) responsibility and accountability for developing an appropriate ITAM implementation approach. Reading this entire guide should be one of their required tasks and they should follow the appropriate steps in Chapter 13 about how to start.

To safeguard the progress of your ITAM initiative

■ **Responsibilities and policies** Establish clear overall responsibilities (with accountability) and policies for ITAM that are commensurate with the degree of centralization considered appropriate. Responsibilities should include risk management for contractual and legal risks. Policies should make clear the obligations of all officers, employees and contractors and the consequences of violations. These policies and their enforcement should be consistent with other policies in use within the organization (e.g. HR policies and information security policies; see Chapters 8 and 9).

■ **Skills and competence** Develop and maintain strong ITAM skills, including those relating to asset lifecycle management and software licensing. Determine whether this is best done in-house, outsourced or by using a hybrid approach. Ensure that your personnel read and understand software licensing contracts, with particular focus on volume-licensing contracts that give audit rights to software publishers. If reliance is being placed on an outside organization, that organization must provide input into all necessary ITAM processes and not just advice on licences for new software being purchased. Remember also that legal exposures cannot be contracted out, so there must be enough internal competence to ensure adequate controls over these exposures (see sections 6.5.1 and G.3.2).

■ **Trustworthy data** Create and maintain accurate inventories of software and hardware assets, including costs; effect secure control over access to software assets (e.g. proof of licence and distribution copies of software; see section 10.3.2). Define targets for data completeness and accuracy and ensure that these are monitored and achieved (see section 7.3.4).

■ **Costs, cost savings and return on investment (ROI)** Monitor costs and savings, and also performance against plans (see section 7.3.3).

■ **Self-review and improvement** Plan and perform regular self-reviews of processes and inventories to ensure that processes are both appropriate and continually improved and that the data maintained is accurate, complete and up to date.

1.3 SOFTWARE ASSET MANAGEMENT AND IT ASSET MANAGEMENT DEFINITIONS

Definitions

Software asset management (SAM)

All the infrastructure and processes necessary for the effective management, control and protection of the software assets within an organization, throughout all stages of their lifecycles.

Hardware asset management (HAM)

All the infrastructure and processes necessary for the effective management, control and protection of the IT hardware assets within an organization, throughout all stages of their lifecycles.

IT asset management (ITAM)

All the infrastructure and processes necessary for the effective management, control and protection of the IT assets within an organization, throughout all stages of their lifecycles.

Note that the definitions are nearly equivalent. See the main text for clarification of the differences.

Within this guide the term 'SAM/ITAM' is frequently used, or the phrase 'SAM and ITAM', because both terms are frequently used in practice, and this guide is not attempting to change that usage. Sometimes the term ITAM is used by itself, especially in diagrams, where ITAM is understood to include SAM. Where the term SAM is used by itself, it indicates a focus on licence compliance, again because that reflects common usage.

Within this guide the term 'IT asset' principally refers to:

- **Hardware** All the physical equipment required to support the provision of IT services, including servers, file storage systems, network components, environmental equipment, etc.
- **Software** All the software required to support the provision of IT services, including applications software, firmware, fonts, systems software, source code, etc. All sources of software are covered, including commercial/proprietary, open-source, and those developed in house.
- **Services** All the services that are related to the provision or support of hardware and software assets, including cloud services such as 'Software as a Service' and those used for maintenance.
- **ITAMS** The IT asset management system itself, including data about all IT assets.

These assets may be on- or off-premises, physical or virtualized, and owned (or not) by the organization.

Non-software digital assets are not considered within the scope of this publication. For example, we do not cover the management of collections of documents, films, recordings and data such as contact databases. Nonetheless, some of the guidance may still be relevant to such digital assets, particularly when licensing is involved.

There are often overlaps between what are perceived as hardware and software assets. For example:

- Hardware functionality is increasingly implemented in software, going beyond simple firmware to concepts such as software-defined storage, software-defined networks and software-defined data centres. Likewise, some software functionality such as security and graphics processing is increasingly implemented in hardware.

■ Media may be considered to be either physical or digital. Physical media will typically hold software and non-software digital assets.

The IT infrastructure comprises the full set of IT assets. In principle, ITAM should include data centre infrastructure management, although in practice it is not understood in that way. This is consistent with the discussion of SAM/ITAM roles in the next section and their typical focus on client-side rather than server-side computing.

All the information required to manage IT assets should be stored in an ITAM database, which should form the foundation of an IT asset management system (ITAMS). The ITAMS should include comprehensive information on all IT assets. The ITAMS could be considered to be a component of the overall service knowledge management system (SKMS), which supports all IT and ITSM areas, practices and processes. The interrelationships between the ITAMS and all the ITSM areas, practices and processes, as defined by ITIL, are explained in Chapter 2.

1.4 NAMING THE ROLE: SAM OR ITAM

There are a number of different ways in which the ITAM role can be named, primarily related to how the organizational structure and responsibilities for software and hardware assets are defined:

■ **ITAM only** If ITAM is the only role defined, it should have responsibility for SAM and for all related hardware (which can be referred to as HAM).

■ **ITAM and SAM** If ITAM and SAM are defined separately, ITAM will tend to have responsibility for hardware only.

■ **ITAM over SAM and HAM** ITAM may also be a role to which there are separate reporting lines for SAM and HAM.

As for SAM, the scope of the HAM role is typically focused on user- or client-side hardware, as distinct from server-side hardware. This can include printers, PCs, tablets, phones and other end-point devices.

There may be functional units which handle sub-groupings of these responsibilities. For example, separate units for client management, mobile device management (MDM) and infrastructure management (including printers). In such cases, the SAM and ITAM names may not be in use, the responsibilities being covered by the related functional roles.

As discussed in section 1.2, SAM and ITAM are required on the server side but typically not given the role names of SAM and ITAM. Licence management responsibilities are often taken by application management teams, while responsibility for hardware management may lie with infrastructure management or ITSM roles.

One of the major trends in recent years is the commoditization of IT, together with a move to further centralize some of the more technical roles, as embodied by the move to cloud computing, which removes the need for much local server-side support. The demands for client-side management, however, continue to increase, as seen in 'bring your own device' (BYOD) developments. This puts increasing demand on the 'traditional' roles of SAM and ITAM.

1.5 ITAM OBJECTIVES AND PROCESS OVERVIEW

Objective

The overall objective of ITAM is to realize value from the use of IT assets by the effective management, control and protection of an organization's IT assets, including management of risks arising from the deployment and use of those assets.

The effective management of software and IT assets is dependent upon the establishment of an effective overall management system. A schematic diagram of an ITAMS is given in Figure 1.2.

Definition: Management system

A management system is the framework of policies, processes and procedures used to ensure that an organization can fulfil all tasks required to achieve its objectives.

Note: Definition taken from ISO management system standards.

Within the ITAMS there are three process groups, each relating to a specific area:

■ **Management system processes for ITAM** These help to govern and manage ITAM overall, and the ITAMS itself, including its supporting processes and activities.

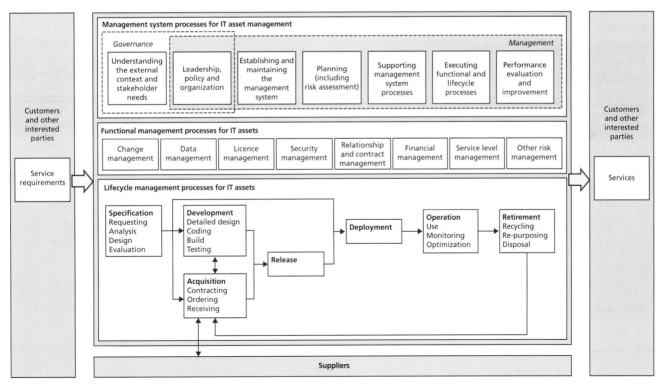

Figure 1.2 The IT asset management system (ITAMS)

■ **Functional management processes for IT assets** These provide management and execution of processing within their specific functional areas, and support interaction with management processes in other areas of IT and the business.

■ **Lifecycle management processes for IT assets** These manage the assets over their lifecycles, from acquisition through to retirement and disposal.

These process groups and processes are described in greater detail in Chapter 10.

An ITAMS can be used within an organization not only to establish effective and efficient processes and activities but also to encourage and drive collaboration, integration and consistency within departmental areas such as ITSM, security and non-IT asset management, thereby helping to break down silos and barriers.

Key message
It is impossible to implement an effective ITAM process without the successful design, development, implementation and maintenance of an ITAMS, together with an underpinning set of accurate, complete and reliable data that is updated on a timely basis, including for replicated instances.

1.6 THE IT ASSET LIFECYCLE

Definition: The IT asset lifecycle
The IT asset lifecycle is the series of stages that IT assets go through during their lifetime.

Different types of IT asset may have different lifecycles. Therefore, one of the early activities of any SAM/ITAM initiative is to define and agree the sequence of stages within the lifecycle for each individual type of IT asset. This will then provide a framework for the design and development of an appropriate set of IT asset lifecycle management processes. The IT asset lifecycle starts with the identification of the need for a new asset and terminates with its eventual disposal.

Context: IT service management and IT asset management

2

2 Context: IT service management and IT asset management

The most commonly used ITSM guidance materials are contained in ITIL and in the ISO/IEC 20000 standard. ITIL is a distillation of best-practice guidelines on the approach, processes and activities required for the effective management, support and delivery of quality IT services. This section briefly describes how ITAM fits with ITIL.

One of the key observations about the relationship between ITAM and ITIL is that ITAM is infrastructure management, whereas ITIL is about service management. The two are intimately connected, but the perspective is slightly different.

IT infrastructure definitions

ITIL defines IT infrastructure as all the hardware, software, networks, facilities, etc. that are required to develop, test, deliver, monitor, control or support applications and IT services.

ISO ITAM defines IT infrastructure as the combined set of IT assets for developing, maintaining and using IT services.

This guide clarifies that the full set of IT assets is the IT infrastructure (see section 1.3).

Table 2.1 ITIL core processes

Core ITIL publication	Processes described
ITIL Service Strategy	Strategy management for IT services
Guidance on how to view service management as both an organizational capability and, more importantly, as a strategic asset. It describes the principles underpinning the practice of service management which are useful for developing service management principles, policies, guidelines and processes across the service lifecycle.	Service portfolio management
	Financial management for IT services
	Demand management
	Business relationship management
ITIL Service Design	Design coordination
Guidance on the design and development of services and service management practices. It contains information on design principles, policies and methods for realizing strategic objectives from a portfolio of services and service assets.	Service catalogue management
	Service level management
	Availability management
	Capacity management
	IT service continuity management
	Information security management
	Supplier management

Table continues

Table 2.1 *continued*

Core ITIL publication	Processes described
ITIL Service Transition Best practices for the planning, transition and support of change. It provides guidance on managing the complexity related to changes to services and service management processes, focusing on desired outcomes and minimizing undesirable impacts.	Transition planning and support **Change management** **Service asset and configuration management** **Release and deployment management** Service validation and testing Change evaluation Knowledge management
ITIL Service Operation Guidance on achieving effectiveness and efficiency in the delivery and support of services to ensure value is realized by users, customers and the service provider. Information is also provided on maintaining stability in service operation, allowing for changes in design, scale, scope and service levels.	Event management Incident management Request fulfilment Problem management Access management
ITIL Continual Service Improvement Creating and maintaining value for customers through all stages of the service lifecycle. It combines principles, practices and methods from quality management, change management and capability improvement for establishing an environment that encourages and facilitates the delivery of continually increasing value.	Seven-step improvement process

More information on the ITIL lifecycle stages and their processes can also be found in *Introduction to the ITIL Service Lifecycle (2011)*.

2.1   WHERE SAM AND ITAM ARE COVERED IN ITIL

2.1.1   Core ITIL

The ITIL core set consists of five publications. Each of these describes a stage within the service lifecycle and provides the guidance necessary for the adoption of an integrated approach to the management of IT services. The five core publications and the processes they describe are listed in Table 2.1. The ITIL processes with most relevance to ITAM are highlighted in bold.

Key message

SAM and ITAM are not sub-processes of service asset and configuration management (SACM). The SACM ITIL process corresponds largely to just one SAM/ITAM process, that of data management.

2.1.2 Extended ITIL

ITIL Practitioner Guidance (2016) provides context and direction for the five core publications as ITIL continues to evolve. It describes and explains nine guiding principles, which are listed here with comments where particular focus is given in this guide. In all cases, however, the principles are of similar importance for both ITAM and ITIL. Reference should be made to *ITIL Practitioner Guidance* for all of them:

- **Focus on value** This is the most important principle of ITSM and ITIL. Everything that a service provider does should, directly or indirectly, lead to value or to increased value for customers, users or the organization.

 Focus on value is of paramount importance to ITAM, as discussed in Chapters 6 and 7. Both ITSM and ITAM practitioners may also benefit from the methodology in *Management of Value* (Office of Government Commerce, 2010).

- **Design for experience** As well as increasing value, the service provider should also focus on continual improvement of the user and customer experience.

 The balanced scorecard approach to selecting metrics helps to ensure that the customer experience remains a focus for management (see section 7.4).

- **Start where you are** Look at what already exists: it is likely that there are things in place that are useful and can be built on.

 This principle is of similar importance for both ITAM and ITIL, with a particular concern for ITAM relating to tool selection.

- **Work holistically** No system stands alone. Ensure that new methods and mechanisms integrate with existing ones.

The ITAMS following the ISO management system approach must be designed with an understanding of its context (see section 10.2).

- **Progress iteratively** Resist the temptation to do everything at once. Break large tasks down into smaller 'chunks' that can be more easily developed and established.

 Following an incremental approach is considered to be a critical success factor (CSF) for ITAM (see section 7.5.1).

- **Observe directly** Monitor and measure progress directly. Base decisions on accurate and trustworthy data.

 Having trustworthy data is considered a CSF for ITAM (see sections 7.5.1 and 7.3.4).

- **Be transparent** Make everything as transparent as possible. The more that people can see what is happening, the more likely they are to help rather than hinder.

 This is an essential aspect of sustainability for SAM/ITAM (see section 7.7).

- **Collaborate** Work with as many areas as possible. The more people that are involved in activities in the right way(s), the greater the chance of success.

 Collaboration is essential for SAM/ITAM projects not only in the short term but in the longer term, where it is a prerequisite for sustainability (see sections 7.7 and 8.5).

- **Keep it simple** Eliminate all waste, duplication and activities that deliver no value. Ensure that all methods and mechanisms are simple, effective and deliver value.

 This rule is particularly relevant to the choice of data to be held about IT assets (see sections 2.3 and 7.3.4).

These nine guiding principles should be adopted by all ITAM projects and programmes to ensure that ITAM activities are consistent and integrate with all other areas, especially ITSM practices.

One way of summarizing much of the advice in *ITIL Practitioner Guidance* is to say that it focuses on 'attitude'. ITSM does not have a mechanistic formula for processes which can be blindly followed; rather, it requires an open, observant, adaptable and pragmatic attitude. ITAM likewise requires this. ITAM must integrate with the rest of IT. If an ITAM practitioner takes a 'blinkered' attitude to their work (i.e. performing their narrowly defined job such as licence compliance without attempting to support the entire organization), they may achieve short-term success but will almost certainly fail in the longer term.

2.2 OVERALL INTEGRATION OF SAM/ITAM WITH ITIL

All ITIL processes are relevant for SAM/ITAM; for example, SAM/ITAM needs to consider strategy and service portfolio, just as ITIL does. The previous section with its list of the ITIL core processes highlights those which are particularly relevant for ITAM. However, the main focus of this guide is on the additional and more explicit requirements of ITAM, such as for licence management.

2.3 HOW ITIL AND ITAM DATABASES RELATE TO EACH OTHER

While ITIL provides a comprehensive framework for ITSM, its databases and repositories can be considered the 'glue' which facilitates the integration of ITIL processes. Databases and repositories also form the foundations of SAM/ITAM,

and are one of the main drivers for integration between the different silos in IT. The success of ITAM is dependent upon data that is accurate and trustworthy (see section 7.5.1). A significant contributor to achieving this is by ensuring that ITAM information and data are integrated and consistent with other similar databases.

The main ITIL databases, repositories and related management systems that are relevant to ITAM are the configuration management databases (CMDBs) within the configuration management system (CMS), the definitive media library (DML) and the overall SKMS.

Of these, the CMDBs are of most interest. Each component recorded within these databases is referred to as a configuration item (CI). Each CI record contains the attributes and information relating to a component, system or service that is necessary for its management. A CMS maintains one or more CMDBs, each of which stores attributes of CIs and their relationships with other CIs.

ITAM inventories and registers are examples of CMDBs. Typically, they are the initial data repositories established by an organization, and often provide the basis for developing ITSM databases.

Key message

Data should only be collected and stored if the value of the data is greater than the effort involved in collecting and maintaining it.

Detailed information and relationships should only be recorded where they add value. Record no more information than is needed to manage assets effectively and realize value from them.

The highest-level concept, the SKMS, is the overall set of tools and databases that is used to manage knowledge, information and data. The SKMS includes the CMS as well as other databases and information systems. The SKMS also contains the tools for collecting, storing, managing, updating, analysing and presenting all the knowledge, information and data that an IT service provider will need to manage the portfolio of IT services throughout their lifecycles.

The DML is much more than a media library, and should be considered as the store or repository not only for both physical and electronic media but also for all documentation and documentary records (such as invoices and licence documentation), again, both physical and electronic. As regards media, the DML acts as a single logical storage repository for all master images or copies of software in use, or planned for use, within the organization, including source code if held.

Further guidance about the integration of ITIL and ITAM databases is given in Chapter 11, together with explanations about variations in the terminology used by ITSM and ITAM practitioners.

2.4   ISO/IEC 20000-1

ISO/IEC 20000 is the multi-part international standard for ITSM. The current edition of Part 1 is from 2011 (ISO/IEC 20000-1:2011), which contains the set of service management system requirements against which an organization can be audited. It is in the process of being revised to conform to the new ISO requirements for all management system standards (MSSs), in a similar way as the ITAM standard has already been revised (ISO/IEC 19770-1:2017). The details within this section apply to the 2011 edition.

The processes contained within ISO/IEC 20000-1:2011 are aligned with and similar to those contained within ITIL. The ITSM system consists of three process areas:

- **Management system processes** These provide management, leadership, direction and commitment to ITSM activities, ensuring that policies, plans and objectives are communicated and understood. They are similar in content to the management system processes for ITAM described in section 10.2.
- **Design and transition of new or changed services** These provide the processes and activities for the design, development and transition of major changes, such as the implementation of a changed or new service.
- **Service management processes** These are the specific processes for the effective provision of quality IT services. The processes within this area are similar to those with similar names within ITIL.

Context: SAM/ITAM and other types of asset management

3

3   Context: SAM/ITAM and other types of asset management

ITAM is just one type of asset management. This chapter considers other types of asset management and how they relate to ITAM. The types to be considered in this chapter are:

- physical asset management
- infrastructure asset management for automated systems (in connection with infrastructure control systems)
- data centre infrastructure management (DCiM)
- intangible property management
- management of information as an asset.

3.1   PHYSICAL ASSET MANAGEMENT

The standard for physical asset management is ISO 55001. As stated in its scope clause, 'This International Standard is intended to be used for managing physical assets in particular, but it can also be applied to other asset types.'

There is no explicit provision in ISO 55001 for dealing with software, licensing or other specific characteristics of IT assets. Annex C in Edition 3 of ISO/IEC 19770-1 explains these differences. Edition 3 takes effectively 100 per cent of the requirements text from ISO 55001 and adds requirements which address the specific characteristics of IT assets.

3.2   INFRASTRUCTURE ASSET MANAGEMENT FOR AUTOMATED SYSTEMS

Infrastructure asset management for automated systems is similar in concept to physical assets as covered by ISO 55001, except that the professional organizations involved address the importance of IT in these assets and in the management of these assets. This area of asset management is more commonly referred to under the label of industrial control systems (ICS) or operational technology (OT) as distinct from information technology (IT).

There is strong focus in this discipline on security, particularly of critical infrastructure. Two significant organizations involved in this area are the US government's Industrial Control Systems – Cyber Emergency Response Team (ICS-CERT), and the International Society of Automation (ISA) and its security subcommittee (ISA/99).

3.3   DCIM

DCiM is a term given to the management of data centre assets including those of a mechanical and electrical (M&E) nature, such as cooling and power distribution systems and occasionally IT assets. DCiM products generally are an enhancement of building management systems (BMS) or energy management systems (EMS) and have a range of modules that can be used to enhance the overall management of the data centre, such as by direct monitoring and control of temperature and humidity within the white space, asset management, capacity planning and energy monitoring/consumption. While this discipline overlaps somewhat with server-side ITAM, its predominant focus is on the physical infrastructure of the data centre, excluding the management of IT processing equipment itself. Where the term 'data centre management' is used elsewhere in this guide (without 'infrastructure'), it includes and indeed focuses on the management of IT processing equipment itself.

Various international standards require the presence of basic DCiM products within the data centre in order to be certified. These include the EN 50600 series of data centre design, build and operational requirements, the ISO 30134 series of data centre key performance indicators (KPIs) and the EU Code of Conduct for Data Centres (Energy Efficiency) Section 9 Measurement and Monitoring.

The Data Centre Alliance at http://www. datacentrealliance.org/ is the data centre trade association addressing this area.

3.4 INTANGIBLE PROPERTY MANAGEMENT

Intangible property or assets include patents, trademarks, copyrights and electronic collections of, for example, media, documents, definitions and credit ratings.

At the time of writing, it is unproven whether either ISO 55001 or ISO/IEC 19770-1 would be suitable for the management of intangible property assets. ISO/IEC 19770-1 would appear more suitable, since it provides for the management of intangible software and associated licences. However, it was developed for an environment where both physical and digital assets need to be controlled.

3.5 MANAGEMENT OF INFORMATION AS AN ASSET

Information, per se, can also be considered an asset. It can be considered as a more generalized case of intangible property assets, described above.

ISO/IEC 27001 (information security management) deals with the management of security over information, but not with the management of information itself. ISO/IEC 27001 requires the creation of an information inventory but gives no direction on how this is to be done, which logically would be a basic requirement of information management itself.

ISO/IEC 19770-1 explicitly excludes from its scope the management of information per se as an asset, because this could extend its scope far beyond what are considered IT assets (e.g. to physical stores of information such as libraries, and to information which people carry in their heads).

It is possible that a new standard or best-practice guidance will need to be developed to deal with the management of information as an asset. One possible approach, in development at the time of writing, is the proposed ISO 30401 Human resource management – knowledge management system – requirements.

Context: the
challenge of change

4

4 Context: the challenge of change

4.1 CHANGE HAPPENS

The world of IT continues to change. Some changes are driven by developments which improve control, such as standardization, commoditization of many aspects of IT, and even some legislation and regulation. However, most changes in IT (both in technology itself and in associated business practices) are driven by forces disruptive for control purposes.

> 'The only thing that is constant is change.'
> Heraclitus

4.2 PERVASIVE SPREAD OF IT

Irrespective of the specific technologies involved, IT is spreading pervasively into almost all aspects of life. The challenge for SAM/ITAM practitioners is whether they will remain siloed in the legacy IT environment (however much updated technologically) or, likewise, spread beyond it. Some of the main examples of these expanded areas are:

- **Management of capital assets and infrastructure** This includes:
  - 'traditional' management of capital assets, such as manufacturing and mining equipment, and other assets such as buildings, vehicle fleets and construction equipment. There are closely related disciplines such as maintenance management, property management and facilities management.

  - management of infrastructure assets such as utilities (e.g. energy, water and telecommunications) and transportation (e.g. railroads, air transport and road transport).

  These are increasingly being automated, both for monitoring and for control. The exposures to cyber-attacks perhaps have the most public focus, but the more significant ones are probably to human error and poor control. SAM/ITAM should be fully relevant in these areas.

- **Internet of Things** (IoT) There is much hype about IoT, but it is definitely coming. The number of internet-connected devices (almost always with some software or firmware included) will grow exponentially faster than anything we have experienced to date. SAM/ITAM should be fully relevant in these areas, both in design (manageability and licensing by design, just like security by design and privacy by design) and in operational management, including patch management.

- **Mobile computing** Mobile devices already dramatically outnumber traditional IT equipment such as PCs and servers. Significant effort is being invested to control this phenomenon in the enterprise space (discussed in Chapter 11) in contrast to what is happening in the small and medium enterprise (SME) and consumer spaces (e.g. for ensuring the patching of insecure versions of mobile device operating systems).

Some of the more encouraging developments to help bring good SAM/ITAM disciplines to these areas are:

■ **Legislation, regulation and national guidance** Critical infrastructure, in particular, is becoming subject to requirements which will help to bring better control and protection (see Chapter 5).

■ **Standardization** Many standardization bodies are working to facilitate control in these areas of growing concern. At times, it appears that these bodies are as competitive as commercial organizations, which could be a positive attribute but tends to make achieving consensus on standards rather difficult.

■ **Cross-discipline communication and cooperation** Many of the industry groups working in these respective areas are increasingly aware of, and working with, each other. But the silo effect is still strong.

4.3 INCREASING CONCERNS ABOUT SECURITY

As IT becomes more pervasive, so do security exposures. SAM/ITAM practitioners should be key participants in efforts to improve security. This is such an important topic that an entire chapter of this guide is devoted to it (see Chapter 14).

4.4 TECHNOLOGY SHIFTS

Changes in technology are some of the major drivers of change in the disciplines and practices of SAM and ITAM. Three major technology shifts are behind the majority of these impacts:

■ **Shift to virtualization** Virtualization is particularly pervasive in the data centre, but it also exists on the client side, whether through use of local virtual machines or virtualized desktops run on central servers. The impacts of this shift include:
  ● the need for more specialist skills for managing virtualized environments, and for managing the associated licensing
  ● the need for better tools able to discover, monitor and manage virtualized environments.

■ **Shift to a cloud-based (virtual) infrastructure** The impacts of this shift include:
  ● greater concentration of specialist server-side skills in third-party data centres, reducing the level of in-house skills required of this type. (SAM/ITAM practitioners have traditionally had less involvement on the server side.)
  ● greater commoditization of IT services, including hardware and also software as provided by cloud service providers. This effectively reduces the in-house skills required to support related hardware and software, transferring in-house responsibilities more towards end-user support and the management of end-user devices and more complex licensing.
  ● greater focus in-house on supporting end-users in cloud-based environments (e.g. virtual desktop infrastructure (VDI) or Software as a Service [SaaS]). SAM/ITAM practitioners have tended to be more involved in these types of activity.

■ **Shift to mobile computing and BYOD scenarios** The impacts of this shift include:

- potential legal issues related to ownership, responsibilities and exposures between the organization, partners and users over devices, applications and data (see section G.3.3 for a discussion of these issues).
- the use of tools for MDM. SAM/ITAM practitioners often are involved in the use of these tools, giving them a greater scope of responsibilities than previously held (see Chapters 8 and 11).

These shifts are also consistent with more reliance on outsourcing and managed services (see section 8.4 and Appendix G).

4.5 CLOUD SERVICE DISCOVERY

As a result of the technology shifts discussed above, a major issue has arisen: that of the increasing use of cloud services by individuals who bypass normal IT procurement procedures. Responsibility for discovering who is making use of cloud services is likely to be assigned to SAM/ITAM. It will be concerned with discovering which cloud services are being used, and in particular with identifying usage of services that were previously unknown to the IT department.

The situation is analogous in some ways to what happened before the development of the current generation of discovery tools for identifying software installed on known equipment. That situation was hard to control, and only improved as better 'local' discovery tools were developed to identify such situations, and more effective techniques were developed to prevent unauthorized installations. In a similar way, we now need better tools for discovering cloud services.

The discovery of cloud services unknown to IT (as opposed to the auditing of cloud services which are already known) is, at the time of writing, primarily based on administrative approaches (e.g. the review of credit card billings) and cumbersome technical approaches, such as the review and interpretation of internet logs. We can expect to see significant advances in the area of discovery and also in control; for example, in auditing actual usage (requiring content analysis) for billing verification, and for planning and justifying future use. It is likely that artificial intelligence will be helpful in these developments (see also section 4.12).

Cloud service discovery should not be confused with 'serverless' cloud services, also known as Function as a Service (FaaS). These services potentially remove the need for the customer to discover, track or manage cloud-based hardware and software assets on the server side. In a fully automated serverless environment the customer has no access to either the underlying hardware or software assets and only pays for the resources consumed, which leaves the provider with responsibility for managing them. These serverless cloud services may still need to be discovered, for example if they have been contracted by an end-user department without the IT department's knowledge.

4.6 DEVELOPMENTS IN LICENSING

There is a general view that software licensing continues to get more complex. This is not necessarily true; there have been some moves to simplify it, such as by reducing the number of upgrade options or via cloud-based SaaS, which generally has a reasonably simple licensing model. However, the trade-off for simplicity is cost, because publishers generally wish to maintain or increase revenues, not reduce them.

Key message

Good cost options generally go together with licensing complexity and require close control, even in the cloud.

A licensing-related consideration is that, since the financial crash of 2008, software publishers are increasingly relying on audits as major revenue drivers. As a result, the majority of medium to enterprise-sized organizations can expect to be audited by at least one publisher every year. Licence compliance audits often result in large unbudgeted costs to organizations, so licensing exposures typically have increasing visibility to top management and the board (see also section 4.7).

Much of the complexity associated with licensing results from the rate of change in virtually all aspects of licensing itself and with technology. In particular, changes in licensing models and metrics are often significantly behind what changes in technology permit. Related areas are also in a state of flux (e.g. the products available for purchase, the licensing programmes under which they are available, and their pricing structure), a situation that is unlikely to change in the foreseeable future.

There are major developments in ITAM standards which will facilitate the automation of control over IT assets, and especially of licensing. These are the technological enablers described in Appendix D, including in particular the software identification tag and the entitlement schema.

It is impractical for most organizations, even for those most likely to experience repeated licence compliance audits, to maintain all the detailed licensing skills in order to have reasonable assurance of licence compliance for all publishers. As a result,

there is increasing reliance on outsourcing, or managed services, to provide licensing expertise (see section 8.4 and Appendix G for more information).

4.7 DEVELOPMENTS IN PUBLISHER AUDIT APPROACHES

In an attempt to minimize the disruption and potential ill will caused by point-in-time audits, some publishers are trying new approaches to achieve their objective of continued licence compliance. The common factor in these programmes appears to be a more frequent but less invasive approach to monitoring, particularly for larger customer organizations. One such approach involves the use of publisher monitoring tools, which may operate continuously. An alternative approach is for the regular involvement of trusted third parties in the preparation or review of licence compliance reports, and the sharing of this information with the publishers. Such approaches may give the publishers considerable inside information, but arguably it is no more than a good dedicated sales representative would learn in any case.

4.8 LEGISLATION AND REGULATION

Legislation and regulation have increasingly become important drivers for SAM/ITAM, and their amount and scope are likely to increase over time. The degree to which a particular organization is affected obviously depends on the legal jurisdiction and on any relevant regulatory authority (e.g. stock exchange or industry regulator). Multinational organizations may need to comply with legislation and regulations from multiple jurisdictions and regulators. Furthermore, national political realignments, such as the UK leaving the EU, are likely to result in significant changes that will be important for SAM/ITAM.

Some of the principal types of legislation and regulation concern the following (see also Chapter 2):

- **Security** Increasingly, security requirements can have an impact on SAM/ITAM. For example, critical infrastructure providers, the financial services sector and pharmaceutical companies typically have mandated security requirements which relate to IT assets.
- **Personal data protection** Mandatory requirements concerning personal data or 'personally identifiable information' are becoming more common. For example, the European Union's General Data Protection Regulation (Regulation (EU) 2016/679) will take full effect from 25 May 2018. One aspect of this legislation is that monitoring information is considered to be personal data; therefore, there could be issues where software usage is being monitored for licence harvesting purposes, if that information could be interpreted as being for personnel assessment purposes. Employment terms and conditions may need careful review.
- **Corporate governance** Many stock exchanges have corporate governance requirements which typically specify compliance with legislation, regulation and contractual commitments (usually including software licence compliance).
- **Cost efficiency** There can even be regulations relating to cost efficiency, especially for governmental and quasi-governmental organizations. For example, the US federal government has the Making Electronic Government Accountable by Yielding Tangible Efficiencies ('Megabyte') Act.

4.9 BUSINESS DRIVERS

Strong business drivers with a distinct risk management element (including for reputational risk) are increasingly affecting SAM/ITAM. In particular:

- **Software licence compliance** The huge financial impact which licence compliance audits can have means SAM increasingly has a fairly high priority with senior management. Unfortunately, the priority is too often exclusively on the avoidance of negative audit results, so the other benefits which should come from good SAM/ITAM are often ignored.
- **Cost savings** Sometimes in reaction to bad results from a software licence compliance audit, there is a strong push for cost savings. These can often be realized, especially via licence harvesting and the termination of unneeded maintenance (see section 6.2).
- **Security** IT security and ITAM should be working in close partnership, although this has yet to become widespread. In particular, the top two critical security controls (CSCs) from SANS (2017) are inventories of (authorized and unauthorized) hardware and software. Reputational risk is particularly important for this driver, because of the extensive negative press coverage which can result from security breaches (see Chapter 14).

4.10 INTERNET OF THINGS

While the Internet of Things (IoT) was mentioned above in the context of the pervasive spread of IT (section 4.2), there are particular issues relating to health and safety for some of these systems, which will inevitably trigger the involvement of SAM/ITAM.

One of the most obvious examples is in the trend for IT systems to be incorporated into vehicles, from 'simple' pollution control and other auxiliary systems to ones that are highly autonomous, such as driverless farm vehicles and cars. This guide sees such systems as an unchartered area for SAM/ITAM in the future.

4.11 BIG DATA

As the data collected by ITAM grows and improves in quality, the approaches used in 'big data' may become increasingly relevant and valuable. For example, big data may drive analytics about when and from where the organization's systems are accessed, for what purposes, and how that information may be used to drive improvements in efficiency, profitability and risk control. This trend will also likely be driven by the increase in digitalization and data collection resulting from the IoT, including sensor devices. Big data could also link into the next topic, artificial intelligence.

4.12 ARTIFICIAL INTELLIGENCE

Artificial intelligence (AI) may have profound and unpredictable effects on IT in the future, and in particular on SAM/ITAM.

Some possible applications include:

- analysing inventories and logs for anomalous situations requiring review and potential intervention or remediation. These could relate, for example, to identifying unauthorized use of cloud services or to misuse of corporate assets (such as exfiltration of sensitive corporate data) by employees. The corresponding threat is that AI could be used by external parties to identify weaknesses in controls.
- analysing licensing entitlements and usage against entitlements in complex scenarios, both to help ensure licence compliance and to identify cost-savings opportunities.
- analysing licensing terms and conditions (e.g. as presented in many click-through agreements when installing software and subsequent updates).
- auditing and analysing usage-based invoices from vendors.
- tracking and analysing data and cloud usage in order to detect complex attack patterns.
- managing much of the IT infrastructure in a semi-autonomous way.

Context:
legal, regulatory and
contractual requirements

5

5 Context: legal, regulatory and contractual requirements

SAM/ITAM operates in a context which has significant exposures in the case of non-compliance with legal, regulatory or contractual requirements. These are based on the legal systems of specific jurisdictions, and it is essential that organizations, and responsible individuals in those organizations, understand the specific requirements that apply to them, and the exposures which exist in the event of non-compliance.

Key message

The protection and enforcement of intellectual property rights, including for software, are increasing worldwide. For example, UK legislation introduced in late 2002 provided for:

- confiscation of assets
- up to 10 years in jail, or
- an unlimited fine.

Although legal, regulatory and contractual requirements may vary by jurisdiction, the following general observations may be made:

- **Legal** Legal requirements are those which are directly specified by legislation. Those which traditionally are most relevant for SAM/ITAM are those associated with trademark and copyright law. These are used by software publishers, and by enforcement organizations when there is an absence of directly enforceable contracts with software publishers. There is legislation in some countries concerning what data may be collected about individuals (e.g. the extent to which individuals may be monitored in their use of IT).

Laws may also exist which deal with issues such as the disposal of IT equipment, the protection of personal data about individuals and requirements for the disclosure of security breaches. Legislation typically also underlies the next two categories of requirements.

- **Regulatory** Regulatory requirements are those which are specified by a regulatory body or a stock exchange. These requirements can be exceptionally demanding for ITAM purposes (for example, in the pharmaceutical industry where poor controls can have life-or-death consequences). Stock exchange requirements are often relevant for ITAM because of their emphasis on good governance and compliance with all relevant laws and regulations. Such regulations often put particular responsibility on individual directors and other officers of the organization. A good source of information about, and links to, corporate governance codes is at www.ecgi.org/codes/all_codes.php.

- **Contractual** Contractual requirements are typically the most significant for ITAM in practical terms, because they provide the main basis for software publisher audits. Outsourcing agreements and cloud service agreements can also create significant exposure if responsibility for licensing and licence compliance is not clearly defined.

Some of the exposures created by these requirements are exacerbated by the nature of supply chains in the IT industry, as explained in Appendix A.

Examples of the scale of the issue

More than 6,500 European businesses were taken to court in a 12-month period for contravention of software copyright.

BSA studies estimate that about 22 per cent of business software used in the UK is unlicensed (2016).

BSA studies estimate that about 39 per cent of business software used worldwide is unlicensed (2016).

There have been many high-profile examples of organizations contravening copyright laws, ranging from high street retailers and international banks, through local government to small- and medium-sized businesses. The penalties for these offences have ranged from a few thousand pounds to hundreds of thousands of pounds.

A national distributor with a chain of several hundred resellers had to pay an undisclosed sum of damages for activities over a number of years where it had been inadvertently distributing counterfeit copies of software that it had purchased in good faith.

Value **6**

6 Value

6.1 THE ROLE OF VALUE IN ITIL AND ITAM

'Quality in a product or service is not what the supplier puts in. It is what the customer gets out and is willing to pay for.' Peter Drucker

Peter Drucker's quote is also relevant here: value is not what you put in; it is what you get out.

The first guiding principle of ITIL is 'focus on value' (see section 2.1.2.) This focus is particularly important for ITAM as well. Indeed, the ISO definition of an IT asset is an 'item, thing, or entity that can be used to acquire, process, store and distribute digital information and has potential or actual value to an organization' (ISO/IEC 19770-1:2017, 3.25).

There are two aspects to value for ITAM, namely the value delivered by the IT assets themselves and the value delivered by ITAM. IT assets deliver value by enabling the organization to deliver its products and services effectively. The value delivered by ITAM goes beyond enablement to include management concerns such as risk management, security, cost control and licence compliance. The focus of this guide, and of this chapter, is on this broader set of values which will result from good ITAM. The areas in which value will be achieved, and the level of value to be achieved, will depend on the scope of assets to be covered by ITAM, the process areas (e.g. as defined by the tiers of ISO/IEC 19770-1:2017), and other factors that are explained in this chapter.

'Value' is a generic concept which includes many other concepts used in association with ITAM, such as benefits, risk management, licence optimization and cost savings. All are covered in this chapter. Value does not exist in a vacuum, but has a cost which must always be balanced against the value to be gained.

The remainder of this chapter discusses the various types of value which can be obtained with ITAM. To facilitate analysis and review, it is useful to have a classification scheme for the types of value which an ITAM programme can deliver. The scheme suggested below attempts to use generally accepted terms; there are, however, alternative ways to describe the different types of value. For example, 'cost savings' may also be described in terms of risk of excessive expenditure. Alternative classification schemes may be used by ITAM practitioners where there is a need to align with other organizational approaches.

The scheme below is ordered practically in terms of quantifiability of value achieved. The subject of security is listed separately from those of cost savings and risk management because in practice it is generally identified separately.

6.2 COST SAVINGS

There are differing views about the meanings of the terms 'cost savings' and 'cost avoidance'. This guide differentiates between cost recovery, cost reduction and cost avoidance, and collectively considers them all to be components of cost savings. Table 6.1 defines and gives examples for each that are taken from the explanations further below.

Table 6.1 Types of cost savings

Type of cost savings	Definition	Examples
Cost recovery	Receiving money (or credit) back for costs already incurred	Intraorganizational billing
		Resale of used licences
		Refunds/credits from vendors/publishers
Cost reduction	Eliminating future obligations for costs currently being incurred and likely to continue to be incurred	Cancellation of unneeded software and hardware maintenance
		Cloud services control
		Licence harvesting and reuse
		Server and architecture restructuring
		Product and infrastructure standardization
		Licence demand management
		Improved commercial terms
		Licensing model optimization
		Improved efficiency and cost-effectiveness
Cost avoidance	Eliminating future obligations (likely and/or possible) for costs not currently being incurred	Reduced project costs
		Reduced strategic infrastructure costs
		Avoidance of underlicensing costs (e.g. as would be identified by a software publisher audit)

All savings figures rely on having good data and information about IT assets and associated costs. Some savings are more difficult to measure, such as those relating to efficiency, where cost attribution can be challenging. The cost of obtaining meaningful value data/information can itself be one of the factors to consider in determining the value of proposed improvements.

Major types of cost savings which can result from improved ITAM include the following:

■ **Intraorganizational billing** Better and more trustworthy ITAM data will facilitate intraorganizational billing. Whether, and how, an organization bills its different units/departments for IT services is generally determined by management policy. Intraorganizational billing results in cost recovery for the IT department but not for the organization as a whole. It may, however, disclose significant discrepancies in the cost/ value of the services, resulting in real savings for the organization.

- **Resale of used licences** Whether used licences can be resold generally depends on licensing terms and conditions (though court decisions in some countries have overridden these anyway).

- **Refunds or credits from vendors/publishers** It might be possible to negotiate refunds or credits from vendors/publishers (e.g. for software which has not performed as expected, or where incorrect products or quantities were purchased as a result of encouragement by vendor/ publisher sales personnel).

- **Cancellation of unneeded software and hardware maintenance** This is typically the easiest 'quick win' to produce significant savings in the short term (see Examples).

- **Cloud services control** Cloud services are typically easy to initiate, including by end-users. However, these services may quickly become problematical for cost control purposes, because they typically renew automatically, even if no longer being used. They also raise operational issues, such as how to ensure data synchronization and security. Close monitoring may reduce or eliminate the cost of services no longer being used or being used ineffectively.

- **Licence harvesting and reuse** Licence harvesting is the reclaiming of software and/or licences from systems (e.g. PCs or servers) where they are not being actively used. Savings are achieved if licences subsequently can be reused elsewhere instead of purchasing new ones. In practice, this frequently provides the most significant financial benefits achieved from an ITAM project, often easily justifying the cost of an ITAM project over several years (see Examples).

- **Server and architecture restructuring** Significant savings are often achievable through server consolidation, involving a switch to fewer but more capable servers. Likewise, a restructuring of client–server architectures, including access rights, can sometimes significantly reduce licensing costs (potentially also avoiding unexpected underlicensing costs identified in a publisher audit) (see Examples).

- **Product and infrastructure standardization** By standardizing on a single (or reduced) set of products, such as word processing and spreadsheet software, unit costs may be reduced, and furthermore support costs may be significantly reduced. This may significantly reduce both server and client costs.

- **Licence demand management** It may be possible to manage licence demand in a way which reduces costs (e.g. by supplying 'readers' rather than 'writers' for PDFs and spreadsheets).

- **Improved commercial terms** Better commercial terms may be obtained (especially lower unit costs) by consolidating multiple existing procurement agreements and by eliminating or reducing retail purchases.

- **Licensing model optimization** Multiple licensing models are often available; for example, client access licences (CALs) may be per device or per user, and sometimes both are used together. Savings are achievable by migrating to a more cost-effective model.

- **Improved efficiency and cost-effectiveness** Almost all processes can be improved through better design. Better information about existing IT assets and how they are used will facilitate better decision-making, which itself drives enhanced efficiency and cost-effectiveness. However, measuring these improvements can be challenging, especially for benefits achieved outside of the IT department.

- **Reduced project costs** The involvement of ITAM personnel in IT projects can significantly reduce project costs by ensuring more cost-effective 'licensing by design', rather than having design decisions taken without recognition of licensing implications.
- **Reduced strategic infrastructure costs** The involvement of ITAM personnel in strategic IT planning can reduce long-term costs by ensuring that licensing implications are properly taken into account.
- **Avoidance of underlicensing costs** Licence non-compliance costs are perhaps the most visible of all ITAM costs, but they are also perhaps the most sensitive to discuss. If the organization has already been audited by a publisher, and needs to pay for licence non-compliance, it is too late to talk about cost avoidance. On the other hand, if underlicensing is identified through an internal review, there may be an issue about how to handle it: correcting the underlicensing, and reporting the costs avoided in management reporting, could trigger publisher demands for payment.

Examples

Client side: Case studies have shown that, typically, more than 35 per cent of software installed on PCs has not been used for 90 days or more, and that the average value for this unused software is more than $240 per employee (1E, 2016).

Server side: Some organizations have reported that 75 per cent of all identified savings are on the server side, with the most significant part of this due to the cancellation of support and maintenance agreements that are no longer required.

6.3 RISK MANAGEMENT

Improved risk management is the second major type of value obtained from good ITAM. This section deals only with the main risks generally cited with respect to IT operations. Improved risk management is also relevant for security and merger/acquisition activity, which are covered in separate sections further below (see also relevant sections in Chapter 10, including in particular sections 10.3.3, 10.3.4 and 10.3.8).

The main events which typically cause risk exposures to materialize as part of regular IT operations are:

- **Publisher audits** Almost all organizations have this risk, and the majority of larger organizations now regularly experience publisher audits. (Section 6.5 gives further details about some of the underlying causes of this risk.)
- **Security breaches** (including unauthorized disclosure of confidential information) Security may be breached because of failure to implement adequate controls, such as: ones to minimize the risk of using non-genuine software (e.g. which may have been tampered with), controls to mitigate the risk of theft/loss of unencrypted mobile devices, or measures for security patch distribution.
- **Data protection breaches** 'Data protection' is a term which refers to the protection of personal information, which is also sometimes referred to as 'personally identifiable information'. A data protection breach is a special case of a security breach, with the potential for extreme impact on the organization. Violations of data protection regulations may incur severe penalties (e.g. European legislation could result in fines of €20 million or 4 per cent of global annual turnover for the preceding financial year, whichever is the greater). In particular, ITAM systems may store

information about users, such as contact information, which may need to be subject to stringent controls. The individuals responsible for data protection in an organization should be consulted to clarify any specific requirements.

■ **Regulatory reviews** Some organizations (e.g. in the financial, pharmaceutical and energy sectors) are subject to regulatory reviews which may include some coverage of ITAM.

■ **Governmental reviews** There are risks in countries or jurisdictions where the legal, tax and regulatory systems are different from those where the organization is primarily based. For example, requirements to pay a local tax on software used can increase costs and complicate practices for software distribution in multinational organizations.

■ **Operational issues and breakdowns** Many risks arise from normal operations, related to when things go wrong.

■ **Negative business developments** Typical business developments, such as suppliers or other partners going out of business, or business conditions deteriorating, always bring a multitude of risks.

The areas where these types of event have their impact are:

■ **Financial risk** Financial risk is typically considered most significant in relation to underlicensing, where the costs involved are not only those of the relevant software but also those of supporting an audit, together with possible penalties from the publisher. Significant financial risk may come from other sources as well, however, such as the imposition of fines or from the impact on the business of system breakdown.

■ **Reputational risk** Because so many organizations have had poor results from software licence audits, poor audit results probably do not present significant reputational risk to the organization unless management was wilful and egregious in its behaviour and ends up in court. However, there can be significant reputational risk to individuals involved in ITAM if they are considered responsible for poor audit results. There can furthermore be significant reputational risk to the organization for unusual occurrences, such as has happened with major interruptions of operations for some banks caused by poorly executed software upgrades.

■ **Legal liability of executive and senior management personnel** Executive and senior management personnel may have personal legal liability for their actions, or inactions, depending on the country/countries, whether the industry is regulated there, and any stock exchanges involved. Responsibilities are generally defined in terms of good governance. A useful source of information is www.ecgi.org/codes/all_codes.php. The exposure for such individuals is potentially major (including prison), but actual cases of this type are rare.

■ **Operational risk** ITAM is potentially associated with operational risk, the most significant being that of interruption of operations, such as may occur through poorly executed software upgrades. Operations may also become unsupportable (e.g. if a publisher goes out of business and the software they provided can no longer be maintained or upgraded). Another type of operational risk is the impact of unexpected workloads, such as might occur when, for example, resources are diverted from a major IT project to work on publisher licensing audits.

The underlying causes for these risks can be many and varied, including failures to implement properly any aspect of good SAM/ITAM as described throughout this guide. However, the causes which should be of most concern to management will typically include:

■ a failure to have or achieve any of the CSFs for SAM/ITAM (see section 7.5.1)

■ a failure to address the causes of software licence non-compliance (see section 6.5).

6.4 ENHANCED SECURITY

There is an entire chapter devoted to ITAM and security (Chapter 14), but it also needs to be mentioned in this list of types of value delivered by good ITAM. Security is often considered as a free-standing issue but it is intricately bound up with good ITAM. MDM is just one of the more obvious areas where ITAM and security need to work together closely.

6.5 SOFTWARE LICENCE COMPLIANCE

Software licence compliance per se is seen by many people as a value in its own right, notwithstanding the implications it has for several other value areas (e.g. controlling costs and managing financial risk). Because of the importance of software licence compliance for most ITAM efforts, this section discusses some of the underlying issues in more depth.

6.5.1 Root causes of software licence non-compliance

There are several root causes of software licence non-compliance. Only the third one of these is controllable by ITAM practitioners:

■ **Characteristics of the software** Software has characteristics which make it intrinsically difficult to control for licensing purposes. These include: the ease with which it can be modified, duplicated and distributed; its technological

complexity (e.g. flexibility of location from which it may be accessed; the number and complexity of components; rate of change; and strong requirement for versioning of components); and the blurred distinction between hardware and software (e.g. firmware and software-defined data centres) (ISO/IEC 19770-1).

■ **Complexity of software licensing** See Appendix B for further details.

■ **Lack of sufficient software licensing expertise** This occurs among both ITAM and non-ITAM personnel. Cases even happen where individuals are so certain of their understanding that they fail to read what is actually written, and are simply wrong as a result. This is the only root cause about which the ITAM project can do something (see sections 7.5.3 and 10.3.3).

6.5.2 Specific causes of software licence non-compliance

Given the root causes cited above, the following are some of the more common specific causes of software licence non-compliance:

■ **Using software (knowingly or unknowingly) without the correct licences being purchased** For example, employees may assume that it is OK to install any software from installation media which the organization owns, because of a lack of awareness about how software licensing and reporting work, and about the limitations on their ability to use that installation media. Likewise, the wrong licence may have been purchased for a product (e.g. an upgrade may have been purchased without having an underlying licence to be upgraded).

■ **Installation of excessive software or options from 'all-options' media** Publishers will sometimes distribute installation media which include both basic software and additional software and/or options that require separate licensing. Support personnel may not understand the licensing implications of installing all the software that is on the media, which at times can have significant cost implications that go unrecognized until the publisher conducts a licence compliance audit.

- **Lack of clarity about responsibility in outsourcer or subcontracting relationships**
Responsibilities for software licensing should always be addressed as part of any outsourcer or subcontracting situation. When these responsibilities are not clearly defined, both sides often assume that the other is responsible, with the result that nobody obtains licences.

- **Software licensing terms and conditions being breached unknowingly** Software licensing terms and conditions are complex, and furthermore vary between different publishers. What is allowed by one publisher may not be allowed by another, and this may cause unexpected breaches. For example, some licences may be moved between affiliated organizations, whereas others may not, creating non-compliance issues when they are moved.

- **Use of pirated software (knowingly or unknowingly)** Increasingly, publishers ensure online activation of software, which means the use of pirated copies is less of an issue than it once was. Nonetheless, it represents an exposure, especially in countries with historically lax attitudes towards copyright enforcement, and in smaller organizations (see section B.6).

- **Loss of proof for licences previously purchased** It is possible that proper licences have been purchased, but that proof has been lost through poor administrative procedures. Various publishers provide online portals to facilitate the tracking of licence purchases, but they may still miss some of them (e.g. those that are made in shops, through companies previously acquired, or with incorrectly recorded company names, such as simple misspellings or because of the use of the department's rather than the company's name).

- **Incorrect reliance on resellers** Resellers sometimes act as intermediaries between software publishers and end-customers. There have been cases where customers rely on reseller invoices and even reseller 'proof of licence', but there is no corresponding purchase by the reseller from the publisher itself. The end-customer should always require the proof of licence issued by the software publisher and not rely on reseller proof. Furthermore, if the reseller consolidates orders from different end-customer locations before reporting to the software publisher, this can create major reconciliation challenges for the end-customer. Such consolidation should not be accepted unless the software publisher licence confirmations are clearly traceable in detail to the individual end-customer locations placing the orders.

6.5.3 Other value from software licence compliance

Software licence compliance does not exist in a vacuum. It requires good controls, which are largely the same as those needed to obtain the other types of value as described in above. An organization which implements good controls, for continuing software licence compliance rather than just occasional point-in-time compliance, should achieve most of the other types of value previously discussed.

Example

A large multinational that had just completed the implementation of ITAM was approached by one of its software publishers with the threat of a licensing audit. The chief information officer (CIO) knew exactly how much of that publisher's software was being used, and where, and even knew that there was over-licensing because of changing IT infrastructures. The CIO immediately agreed to the audit, but the software publisher never conducted it. The CIO's improved view of software usage allowed him to achieve significant cost savings, not only with that software publisher but with many others as well. Significant savings on planned future hardware expenditures were also achieved.

6.6 OTHER TYPES OF VALUE FROM SAM/ITAM

6.6.1 Control over interoperability

Good ITAM controls can help in achieving interoperability. Interoperability between systems is important in general, but it is especially so given the increasing use of cloud computing and the frequently free-standing nature of cloud-based applications. Cloud services control (see section 6.2), which is so important for cost control, can also be used as the basis for improved control over the interoperability of in-house systems and cloud-based systems.

6.6.2 Merger/acquisition/demerger management

Good ITAM delivers value throughout merger and acquisition (M&A) activity, including demergers and selling one's own organization to another. 'Due diligence' work is significantly facilitated. Specific value that can be delivered is:

- **Financial value** There is greater certainty about the inventory of IT assets, and about licence compliance, including any risk of underlicensing.
- **Operational value** Good ITAM facilitates the merging, or demerging, of IT infrastructures and of associated software licences. Merged organizations can become fully operational and the benefits realized more quickly.

6.6.3 Improved overall management

Good ITAM supports improved overall management because it provides trustworthy data for decision-making. For example, contractual negotiations can proceed on the basis of accurate information rather than estimates. This higher-quality information also supports better financial and strategic IT planning.

The most significant value of good ITAM as seen by many managers is that it helps avoid surprises. While bad publisher audit results are one obvious type of surprise which managers wish to avoid, trustworthy data will help to avoid surprises throughout IT and throughout the organization.

6.6.4 Competitive advantage

Good ITAM helps give the organization competitive advantage by facilitating the speedy yet controlled introduction of new products, services and capabilities.

6.6.5 Empowerment

Good ITAM helps empower regular personnel and management to do their jobs more effectively and efficiently; for example, by enabling people to obtain the software they need promptly. Likewise, good ITAM ensures the delivery of its services with a minimum of hassle so staff are not forever being distracted by IT problems.

Examples of value achieved through SAM/ITAM

Note: The examples cited here are realistic examples of what is achievable. The savings in each case were dependent on the specific circumstances of the organizations involved, and on the licensing programmes/pricing relevant for them at the time. Most of the benefits cited here relate to savings in licensing costs, which are often the easiest to identify. However, licensing is only a small part of the total cost of ownership (TCO), and the savings in other areas may easily be much larger, although often harder to quantify.

Multinational organization

A multinational organization had a decentralized approach to software licence negotiations. This resulted in recurring over-purchasing of licences and poor pricing. By centralizing the process of software licence management, consolidating all regional contracts into a global one and having more direct contact with software suppliers and publishers, more cost-effective licence agreements were obtained, saving an estimated $5 million.

Facilities management company

A facilities management company implemented a software scanning tool as part of a SAM/ITAM programme, and found a variety of unapproved software on employee computers, including cracked copies of popular office suites, peer-to-peer file-sharing clients and computer games. The impact on security, compliance and employee productivity was hard to measure, but deemed significant.

Large organization

A large organization needed to upgrade its software. Prior to implementing SAM/ITAM, its best alternative was to purchase a site agreement covering usage on all machines. After determining what licences it owned, it was found that the organization needed to purchase only upgrade licences, achieving their objective at only 46 per cent of the cost of the site agreement.

Financial services firm

A financial services firm was able to strengthen its bargaining position with its largest software publishers by having a clear view of which software was required and which would be supporting the strategic IT plan in the future. Prior to having good ITAM data, such insight would have been unavailable or inaccurate, and they would have been forced to sign expensive blanket agreements with the publisher.

Maintenance contracts

A review of software maintenance contracts at an organization revealed that maintenance was continuing to be paid on software that was no longer being used. The contracts were cancelled at a saving of more than half a million euros.

Large service provider

A large service provider faced financial and reputational loss when forced to review SaaS contracts with some of its customers following a software publisher audit. The licensing responsibility for some software products was not clearly stated in contracts. The publisher placed the licensing responsibility with the service provider.

Major company

A major company with a comparatively low PC:employee ratio found that it could reduce its need for CALs by 45 per cent by switching from calculating CALs on a per-person basis to a per-PC basis.

Large bank

A large bank decided to include the SAM/ITAM team in the design phase of new IT projects. The licensing expertise provided IT architects with insight into the cost impact of the licences associated with proposed hardware and software configuration alternatives. When managers were confronted with the costs, some features deemed essential became 'nice-to-haves'. In contrast, some more expensive licence metrics were chosen, because by reducing complexity of measurement and management by the SAM/ITAM team, the overall cost decreased.

Multinational company

A multinational company achieved more than €3.5 million savings on an engineering software suite by implementing a global licence model instead of entity-based local licensing. Application accessibility and variety was also increased significantly to the end-users' satisfaction.

Realizing and
sustaining value

7

7 Realizing and sustaining value

Chapter 6 explains the many types of value which can be obtained from ITAM. Actually obtaining that value, and continuing to obtain it over time, is a typical challenge. This chapter provides guidance on how to meet this challenge in ITAM. Additional guidance is available in *Management of Value* (Office of Government Commerce, 2010).

This chapter is organized into the following sections:

- **Setting priorities** It is not possible to do everything at once. Suggestions are given about setting priorities so as to achieve maximum benefits in the short term while also achieving sustainability.
- **Making the value business case** Guidance on some practical experience in what works, and what does not, in business cases.
- **Measuring value** Guidance on how to measure value, including for both financial and non-financial metrics.
- **Balancing and visualizing value** Guidance on how to make value measurements more effective with management by expressing them via a balanced scorecard.
- **Achieving value** Guidance on CSFs and other issues which are important in determining the level of value which is achieved from ITAM.
- **Communicating value** Guidance on selling the value achieved through ITAM to management and to the overall organization.
- **Sustaining value** Guidance on how to sustain an ITAM programme which delivers value after the 'low-hanging fruit' have been picked.

7.1 SETTING PRIORITIES

It is not possible to achieve everything at once with ITAM any more than with any other discipline. Priorities need to be set which ensure that the immediate objectives of the ITAM programme reflect management's and the organization's priorities, and which will produce meaningful results both in the short term and by providing a path to sustainability for the ITAM programme.

7.1.1 Alignment with organizational and management priorities

The priorities of the ITAM programme need to be aligned with the priorities of the management personnel at least one level higher than ITAM management itself. In other words, the non-ITAM manager to whom ITAM reports must see that ITAM supports that manager's own priorities. It should also be possible to show how these management priorities are themselves aligned with overall organizational priorities. Not everything can be a priority, so choices have to be made. Examples of the types of management priority with which the ITAM programme might need to be aligned, depending on the organizational culture and the individuals involved, are:

- cost reduction
- security
- quality
- software licence compliance
- operational efficiency (e.g. streamlining IT service delivery)

- supporting other initiatives (e.g. a major IT transformation)
- a need to demonstrate good corporate governance of IT
- a need to ensure competent IT risk management
- avoiding surprises
- helping management drive major new technologies while not losing control (e.g. in support of a digital transformation initiative).

7.1.2 Low-hanging fruit

Cost savings are among the most common management objectives for ITAM. The opportunities will differ for each organization depending on its own circumstances. However, the following are typically the major areas of 'low-hanging fruit' for many organizations just starting on an ITAM programme. Even organizations with fairly mature programmes should revisit these areas periodically to ensure that opportunities are not being missed (see also section 6.2):

- **Cancellation of unneeded software and hardware maintenance and support** Identifying such maintenance involves reviews of invoices, and can easily cover both the client and server sides.
- **Licence harvesting and reuse** Benefits typically accrue over a period of 2–3 years and can often be used to fully justify an ITAM programme. The focus of such an initiative is often on the client side.

7.1.3 Ripe fruit further up the tree

There is the potential for even greater savings to be obtained, especially on the server side. The challenge in achieving these benefits, however, is that many ITAM teams focus on the client side and so do not have the expertise or access needed to achieve these savings. If the ITAM programme is properly integrated into all IT, then these opportunities become realistic (see also section 6.2). Particular opportunities for savings may exist in:

- server and architecture restructuring
- licence harvesting and reuse on the server side.

7.1.4 Pathway to sustainability

A common experience for ITAM programmes is that they are severely cut back or even terminated after several years once the easy (but often major) savings have been achieved. To avoid this, the priorities for an ITAM programme need to include steps to achieve long-term sustainability. This is discussed further in section 7.7.

7.2 MAKING THE VALUE BUSINESS CASE

Making a successful value business case is essential for SAM/ITAM, as it is for any other function, and there is considerable general guidance available on preparing one. However, there are a number of special considerations in making the value business case for SAM/ITAM. This section assesses and prioritizes these considerations as has been seen pragmatically to be most effective in preparing such value business cases. The special factors to be considered include, in particular:

- **Publisher audits** Empirically, it appears that most value business cases for SAM/ITAM are approved only after a software publisher audit has resulted in significant unexpected expenditure to correct underlicensing. The resulting formal value business case which is approved tends not to focus on the avoidance of such exposures in the future, but rather on cost savings, as if in reaction to the unexpected costs just incurred. The corresponding observation is that unless management's attention is seized by an outside shock, such as an adverse publisher audit, it is difficult to persuade them to approve even the most well-prepared value business case for SAM/ITAM. Even if a publisher audit is the main reason for approving a SAM/ITAM initiative, and management wishes to recoup its unexpected costs, cost savings from SAM/ITAM typically accrue over a longer timeframe, and it is not usually possible to achieve in short-term cost savings the unexpected immediate costs resulting from a publisher audit.

■ **Cost savings** There is significant potential for cost savings in most organizations which have not previously focused on SAM/ITAM. The areas where savings can be obtained, and the period over which those savings can be achieved, will depend on each organization's specific circumstances, but those most easily quantifiable are often for software licensing and largely result from a reduction of future costs rather than from cuts in current expenditure. Empirically, the biggest cost savings for many ITAM projects have been found in licence harvesting and reuse, as explained in section 6.2. A good understanding of licensing terms and conditions, and good data, are needed to plan for, achieve and demonstrate all these savings. However, publisher resistance can be expected if they see their recurrent revenue streams dropping. Note that cost savings typically are harder to demonstrate after 2 or 3 years, creating a risk of programme cut-back if the value business case is not well built, and the programme has not been designed and implemented in a way which demonstrates continuing value (see section 7.7).

■ **Avoidance of surprises** The avoidance of future unexpected surprises (in the form of major unbudgeted expenditure where underlicensing is found during publisher audits) is one of the key benefits which sell the value business case to senior management. However, as mentioned above, there need to be other, sustainable benefits to justify continuing management support for the SAM/ITAM programme.

■ **Transition project driver** SAM/ITAM does not always need stand-alone justification. It is possible for a SAM/ITAM programme to be effectively embedded into a major transition or change project, such as IT reorganizations, hardware refreshes and hosting provider swaps. This provides an ideal opportunity to reflect on how software is used, and how it is best licensed. The cost of SAM/ITAM is usually minimal in comparison to the overall project budget.

■ **Missed security justification** Potentially the greatest justification for SAM/ITAM is generally not being exploited, because it requires more effective integration with security. In particular, the top three CSCs are all ITAM controls, yet ITAM and security currently have little meaningful integration in most organizations (see Chapter 14).

This being said, a value business case is still required, and the success or failure of a SAM/ITAM project both in the short term and in the long term is highly dependent on how well the value business case is constructed and sold. Successful implementation of SAM/ITAM (including having the right people, processes and tools) is dependent on the commitment and support of business and IT managers. None of these are likely to give their support unless a successful value business case is produced and accepted by senior management. Ideally, this case proves the intangible as well as financial benefits to all the stakeholders.

Key message

It is important to understand the goals and motivation of the people who will approve or reject the SAM/ITAM value business case. If there are key short-term financial targets for cost-cutting, those aspects should be emphasized. If stakeholders have a more visionary approach, the value business case should reflect that.

Senior management and financial approval bodies are not primarily interested in technical arguments. To be successful, a value business case must show the benefits and, if possible, relate costs to future business benefits (ROI), using sound methods of investment appraisal. However, the value business case should also reflect the obligation to comply with contractual and legal requirements, although this might not yield immediate financial returns for the organization.

Often, the value business case for SAM/ITAM is only accepted after a compelling event, such as a negative experience following a software publisher audit. However, financial penalties incurred as a result of an audit might be hard to recover through SAM/ITAM in the short term.

7.3 MEASURING VALUE

7.3.1 General principles

It is necessary in most organizations to have quantitative measures for measuring and monitoring the value delivered. Short-term management imperatives which do not require measurements might be sufficient for a brief period (such as dealing with underlicensing issues), but in the longer term quantitative measures will be needed,

and it might then be too late to start obtaining the necessary data.

Unfortunately, not everything that is important can be measured. For example, the most empirically important CSF for ITAM is executive sponsorship (see section 7.5.1). However, this factor is intrinsically unmeasurable, or only measurable subjectively.

> 'Not everything that can be counted counts, and not everything that counts can be counted.'
> Albert Einstein

While acknowledging that measurement of some factors may be impossible or impractical, we need to measure and control what we can. Metrics are used to give an approximation or indication of the value delivered, rather than necessarily measuring the actual value.

A basic requirement for any metric is to have baseline measurements against which to measure improvement. Consequently, it is important to define metrics as early in an ITAM project as possible, to ensure that relevant baseline data can be obtained. New metrics can be defined at any time, but the extent of improvement demonstrated will be less impressive than it could have been with the earlier baseline.

> 'Measurement is the first step that leads to control and eventually to improvement. If you can't measure something, you can't understand it. If you can't understand it you can't control it. If you can't control it you can't improve it.'
> H. James Harrington (President International Academy for Quality).

Measurable targets, measurements and metrics are key aspects of continual improvement as illustrated by the previous quote. The problem with many organizations is that management reports contain too many measurements, rather than focusing on just a few vital ones. The most important metrics are typically called key performance indicators or KPIs. There is also a related class of metrics called service level metrics (see also section 7.3.6).

In practice, ITAM adds some significant extra requirements for metrics to those typically used in ITSM (which tend to focus only on delivery of services). These are also relevant to ITAM because ITAM provides asset management services. However, there is a particular focus in ITAM on trustworthy data (which is also critical for security) and on licence compliance.

Another issue to consider is how metric targets are expressed. Targets generally can be expressed in absolute terms or in terms of improvement (percentage increase/decrease) from previous performance. ITSM metric targets are often expressed in terms of increases or decreases/reductions. The ISO ITAM standard requires quantitative targets to be specified for data accuracy, which are implicitly absolute targets; similarly, absolute quantitative threshold criteria are specified in some publishers' contracts concerning penalty charges for underlicensing. There is also the issue of intra- and inter-industry comparability of metrics, which requires absolute measures. Consequently, each organization must decide for itself how it wishes to express its metrics, and indeed the same ones can be expressed in both ways, if desired.

Metrics need to be reviewed regularly:

■ to see what should be measured and what can be measured, continually trying to get to what should be measured
■ for context: some measurements and metrics might be more important at particular times of the day, month or year

■ to ensure that they reflect the culture, policies, processes and needs of the organization
■ to ensure they are still relevant and appropriate.

The classifications of metrics in the sub-sections below are aligned with those shown in the balanced scorecard discussed in section 7.4. The classifications and descriptions given are suggestions only. Whether a metric is considered in the 'process' quadrant or in the 'improving and sustaining' quadrant, for example, is particularly dependent on the context and on how objectives are defined. Each organization should determine what is appropriate for itself.

7.3.2 Customer metrics

The customer quadrant is typically the primary quadrant for ITSM. Less detail is given below for metrics in this quadrant, because this is a particular focus of ITIL, to which further reference should be made for guidance on how to define these metrics. Some of the principal ones are:

■ **Service levels** A particularly important service level metric for ITAM is 'mean time to deploy', which is the average time taken from the hardware or software request to the asset being fully usable by the person requesting it, as measured from the perspective of that person. It should typically be broken down (e.g. by deployment type and/or by customer type); see also section 7.3.6.
■ **Customer feedback** This can be measured by several different types of metric, such as:
  ● **Outcomes** This typically records whether the customer request was met (e.g. via a request completion sign-off). It will typically be associated with service level metrics (e.g. how long it took to meet the customer request,

and whether multiple interactions were required before the request was met).

● **Customer experience** This is typically based on feedback to individual transactions (e.g. 'How good was your experience today?').

● **Customer satisfaction** This is generally based on periodic feedback to an ongoing relationship (e.g. via customer satisfaction surveys).

● **Customer complaints** This tends to be based on quantitative and categorized data, as recorded by the service desk.

There are some particular considerations with regard to satisfaction surveys:

■ **Good survey practice** Surveys can provide valuable feedback and also be a way of making people aware of what ITAM is doing. However, they can also generate resistance, partially caused by survey 'fatigue' in general but also because of poor survey design. If you wish to conduct a satisfaction survey, consult with people skilled in such things and do not assume that anyone can conduct a good survey. Also, try to coordinate it with other organizational survey efforts, so you are seen as being a team player.

■ **Need for quantifiable feedback** Request quantitative feedback (e.g. ratings on a scale of 1 to 6); otherwise it is difficult to present meaningful overall results. Free-form feedback and suggestions for improvement will also be valuable, but they are not useful as metrics.

7.3.3   Financial metrics

The following are suggested as generic financial metrics in all ITAM programmes:

■ **ROI** Return on investment for ITAM, or for the ITAM programme, should always be considered when developing such a programme, and in tracking its actual performance. There are

different measures for financial results, as described in section 6.2. Investment may likewise be defined in different ways but should generally include all ITAM programme costs, including those relating to personnel, managed services (e.g. external licensing expertise) and any ITAM-specific tools. It is also desirable to identify separately any costs against non-financial objectives, such as licence compliance.

■ **Savings by type** It is recommended that savings should be identified by type (as given in section 6.2) separately identifying, at a minimum, cost recovery, cost reduction and cost avoidance, and potentially also the types at the lower classification levels. Ideally, savings achieved in the current period (e.g. quarter), in the current financial year and project-to-date (e.g. from the beginning of the ITAM programme) should be reported. A policy should be established concerning how long cost reductions can be claimed. For example, if unneeded maintenance is cancelled, it is probably appropriate to consider it as a saving for one or two entire renewal periods. This is shown in the case study in section 7.5.

7.3.4   Process metrics

The following are suggested as generic non-financial metrics which should be particularly useful in all ITAM programmes; they should also be useful for comparing the results of ITAM programmes between different organizations. Note that the first two together constitute 'data trustworthiness'. They are required by the ISO ITAM standard, which states that ITAM objectives shall 'include quantitative targets for data accuracy'. The metrics about underlicensing may also be needed to assess performance against the contractual terms and conditions of publishers' audit clauses. The process metrics are as follows:

■ **Completeness of IT asset data** Percentage of discovered assets which are already inventoried, by product: for client and non-client devices (e.g. servers and network equipment) separately; for hardware and software separately.

For this metric the discovery process needs to be comprehensive (e.g. to include non-networked and segregated network devices, and virtual machines). Reporting could also include detailed lists of products identified which were not already inventoried.

■ **Accuracy of IT asset data** Percentage of inventoried assets, by product, for which discovered details are inaccurate: for client and non-client devices separately; for hardware and software separately.

Discrepancies should be monitored and reported at the product level, but reflect whether there are inaccuracies at any level of detail for that product, with missed deletions and additions also counted as discrepancies. Note for this metric that it is important to have only useful data in the database.

Key message

A database containing data fields for which there is little use and little incentive to keep up to date will quickly become untrustworthy. Unnecessary fields should either be eliminated from the database, or clearly marked as being of dubious accuracy, both to exclude it from this metric and to prevent data users from relying on it.

■ **Licence compliance** The cost of software usage that is properly licensed compared with costed total usage (i.e. adding in the estimated cost of unlicensed usage), for scope.

Scope for calculations is user-defined, but is typically by software publisher. A typical target might be 96 per cent (based on a possible publisher contractual threshold for penalty pricing of 5 per cent underlicensing). Reporting should also include estimated monetary value of underlicensing. Any underlicensing which cannot be corrected simply by purchasing new licences (e.g. if the product has been discontinued) should be highlighted.

7.3.5 Improving and sustaining metrics

These are metrics which relate either to (a) areas where improvement is almost always needed, as opposed to ones where there is a target which does not need to be exceeded; or (b) to indicators which are key to the sustainability of an ITAM programme:

■ **ITAM integration into IT projects** Percentage of IT projects incorporating ITAM representation.

This metric is useful for demonstrating the degree of integration of ITAM with the rest of IT. There could be breakdowns (e.g. by development and operations, and based on project size).

■ **Authorization** Percentage of discovered assets which are fully authorized: for hardware and software separately. This is effectively a security metric.

Non-authorized devices and software normally should be followed up immediately. Regular reporting could also include detailed lists of hardware and software which were not authorized, and where they were found.

Another security-related KPI might be the number of 'reportable' security incidents caused by ITAM-related failures.

- **Acquisitions from preferred sources** Percentage of software and hardware ordered from a centrally managed and controlled cart of products: by hardware and software; by quantity and by value.

  Acquisitions from the supported hardware catalogue (SHC) may be split into categories of hardware (e.g. servers, laptops, network).

  Acquisitions from the supported software catalogue (SSC) may be split into categories of software (e.g. applications, databases, PCs).

- **Controlled deployments** Percentage of software products deployed using preferred software deployment: for servers and client devices separately; by quantity and by value.

  Reporting could also include detailed list of products deployed using non-standard deployment approaches.

- **Controlled retirements** Percentage of retired products processed using a controlled disposal and reusage process: for servers and client devices separately; by quantity and by value.

  Reporting could provide breakdowns by recycling; re-purposing; and disposal.

- **Risk reduction** Quantitative reduction in the level of risk as calculated by the organization's risk management methodology, for the risks recorded in the ITAM risk register.

7.3.6 Metrics and service levels

There may be significant overlap between the metrics developed for monitoring ITAM overall (especially KPIs), and the service level metrics which are used to define performance targets with customers and suppliers. Those metrics, and the related service level agreements (SLAs) and operational level agreements (OLAs) are covered in the functional management processes of relationship and contract management (see section 10.3.5) and

service level management (see section 10.3.7). Some key observations about similarities and differences are:

- Service level metrics generally define performance targets which should be met, but not exceeded. KPIs tend to be more goal-oriented, with the goalposts typically moving over time.
- Service level metrics may be vendor- or customer-specific, whereas KPIs tend to be more global in nature.
- Service level metrics may often be KPIs, but not all KPIs will necessarily be service level metrics.
- Both service level metrics and KPIs allow for intra- and inter-industry comparability if they are appropriately defined.

Examples of some service level metrics for ITAM are:

- percentage of asset deployments achieved within SLA targets
- number of service performance variances from agreed service levels
- number of complaints related to issues with assets and asset data
- number of non-standard assets deployed (i.e. not from the SHC or SSC).

Corresponding KPIs defined in the way often used in ITSM would be the increase or reduction in these same metrics, compared with the previous period.

7.4 BALANCING AND VISUALIZING VALUE

One challenge associated with measuring value is the need to keep a balanced view. For management purposes, many different measures, metrics or KPIs may be relevant, but an excessive focus on any class of measures will almost certainly be counterproductive overall as other aspects will suffer. For example, a focus on cost savings which ignores the impact on service levels, data trustworthiness and licence compliance will almost certainly result in overall failure for ITAM.

The challenge is to select the most appropriate combination of KPIs to be used. One method that helps to do this is the balanced scorecard (BSC) approach, developed by Kaplan and Norton (1992). This approach proposes the use of four quadrants: customer, financial, process, and improving and sustaining, as shown in Figure 7.1.

The two KPIs in the process quadrant (data trustworthiness and licence compliance) are the most important KPIs for ITAM within many organizations.

In practice, at least one KPI should be selected from each of the BSC quadrants, to provide a balanced approach to the management of ITAM activities. Depending on the organizational and management priorities, different quadrants may have different relative priorities, but they should all be represented. Typically, the customer quadrant will be the

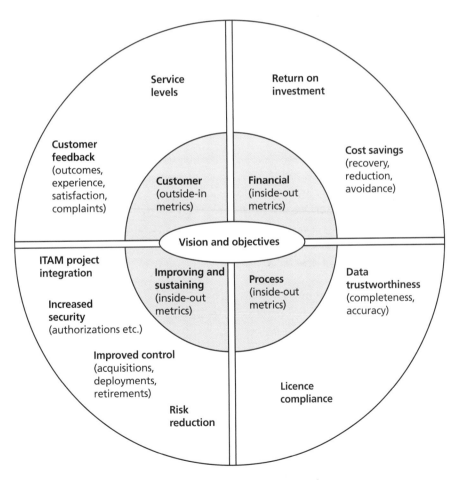

Figure 7.1 Visualizing balanced value using the balanced scorecard

quadrant of primary focus for ITSM. This may be different for ITAM, as licence compliance (in the process quadrant) may be the most important for management, all the way up to the board level. Cost savings may be the second most important, up to the chief officer level.

The KPI(s) chosen within the customer quadrant should be selected in consultation with customers, users and stakeholders, to represent the value required by them from ITAM activities.

Further information on metrics and measurements can be found in Chapter 4 of *ITIL Practitioner Guidance* (2016).

Case study

An internal IT service provider within a FTSE 100 company had implemented most of the ITSM processes throughout its organization. It had achieved certification against ISO/IEC 20000 and wanted to keep focus on continual improvement in the quality of service delivered. Many suggestions were listed in an improvement register, each being prioritized in terms of its value to the business and its alignment with the IT strategy and objectives. From this analysis it was decided that ITAM activities would be the next area of focus. Based on discussions with customers and users, the improvement team submitted a brief business case to the joint business and IT prioritization board. This was approved and an ITAM improvement plan instigated.

The BSC approach was already used by the IT organization so it was decided that a BSC would also be used to measure the progress of the ITAM improvement project. Further discussions were held with customers, users and suppliers/partners and a detailed project plan was produced. The final KPIs selected in each of the quadrants were:

Key message

It is important that ITAM activities aimed at achieving non-customer KPIs do not cause a decline in service levels or in the fulfilment of customer expectations.

Exactly how to show measurements of the chosen KPIs is a separate question. The types of chart that may be appropriate depend on the specific KPIs. However, it is strongly recommended that they always be related back to the BSC for management reporting, to ensure the issue of balance is not lost in the process of presenting results.

- **Customer** Improved service request fulfilment (more successful and faster)
- **Financial** Reduced operational costs
- **Process** Increased licence compliance
- **Improving and sustaining** Increased acquisition of preferred assets.

The main ITAM actions taken were to:

- upgrade tools and increase the use and automation of the IT asset discovery process
- automate identification, removal and recycling of unused and unauthorized software and hardware assets
- review and consolidate partners and contracts for hardware and software
- use preferred assets from an SSC and an SHC, wherever possible
- improve and automate the service request process, using standard, reduced builds and request models of all SSC and SHC assets
- include asset management representation within all major programmes and projects.

During the first 6 months only a few minor improvements were observed in the quality of service. However, in the following 18 months significant progress was made and measured once the tools and processes had been enhanced. These significant improvements included:

■ **Customer** The success rates for service request fulfilments increased from 85 to more than 98 per cent, and fulfilment times reduced from 5 to 2 days for more than 95 per cent of requests.

■ **Financial** Reductions in excess of £650,000 (see Figure 7.2) were achieved through savings in software licensing costs and in contract savings (e.g. cancelled maintenance and better pricing through contract consolidation).

■ **Process** The number of unauthorized assets detected was reduced from the hundreds to less than 20 per month.

■ **Improving and sustaining** More than 85 per cent of all asset purchases made were preferred assets from within the SSC and SHC.

Additional benefits were also detected:

■ The attitude of customers and users to the use and management of IT assets changed.
■ The culture of the whole organization towards the use and management of IT assets changed.
■ Relationships were improved with software publishers and distributors.
■ Exposure to risk was significantly reduced.
■ The security of IT assets and IT systems improved.

The whole project was so successful that:

■ further funding was made available for continued ITAM activities
■ a permanent ITAM role was created.

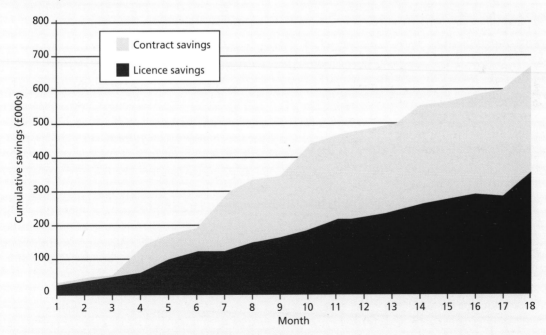

Figure 7.2 Visualizing value: savings in operational costs

7.5 ACHIEVING VALUE

7.5.1 Critical success factors

There are a number of CSFs for successful ITAM:

- **Executive sponsorship** The most important CSF observed for successful ITAM projects is to have strong executive sponsorship. A programme driven purely bottom-up has limited prospects for success because there are too many issues which require strong management support (e.g. in obtaining proper resourcing, and in enforcing policy when some individuals wish to ignore it).

- **Implementation approach** Two CSFs relate to ITAM implementations:
  - **Project approach** ITAM needs to be run as a project, or as a series of projects, with clear objectives for each. ITAM cannot be expected to accomplish change without a clear project focus, which includes responsibilities, accountabilities and deadlines.
  - **Incremental approach** ITAM implementation needs to be done incrementally rather than all at once. This complements the project approach.

Example

A large travel organization was starting an ITAM implementation with adequate people and resources committed to the project. However, overall ownership was not agreed, neither were roles and responsibilities within the implementation of the ITAM processes clearly defined, documented and agreed. The result was that much time was wasted, the project was delayed, and if remedial actions had not been taken, it could have been cancelled.

- **Trustworthy data** Having trustworthy data (i.e. data which is both accurate and timely) is ultimately the criterion on which ITAM succeeds or fails. KPIs should be used to set targets for this, and to provide regular tracking of progress (see section 7.3.4).

- **Ensuring sustainability** For an ITAM programme to be successful in the longer term, it requires particular steps to be taken (see section 7.7).

7.5.2 Variable success factors

A number of other factors have a significant impact on the degree of success which an ITAM project will have, although they do not predict success or failure. We refer to these as variable success factors (VSFs). To the extent that these factors are detrimental in effect, the ITAM project will need to find ways of coping with them. Over time it may also be possible to influence management and the organization to modify the existing approach by demonstrating the impact it has on results.

- **Degree of centralization** This is probably the most significant variable factor affecting the level of value which ITAM can deliver. This is because many of the benefits which ITAM delivers have their greatest potential in a centralized environment, and are hardest to achieve in one that is the opposite. For example:
  - **Standardization** The benefits of standardization are largely determined by the scope of the organization to which they apply. This affects both direct product costs and the indirect costs of operations, support, and training.
  - **Opportunities for consolidation and specialization** Centralization generally provides greater opportunities for both consolidation (e.g. of contracting arrangements) and specialization (e.g.

software licensing expertise). Decentralized organizations encounter the major issue of how to consolidate data from different ITAM systems when publisher audits are invoked for the organization as a whole.

- ● **Opportunities for licence optimization** Centralization generally provides greater opportunities for managing licences cost-effectively. Units which insist on controlling their 'own' licences inhibit the redeployment of unused or underused licences throughout the rest of the organization.

- ■ **Culture regarding policies and enforcement** Senior management's attitude towards what policies are appropriate, and how they will be enforced, is important in ITAM. For example, any organization wants to minimize its exposure to risk. However, the introduction of a policy stating that employees are only allowed to install approved software will be futile if that policy is not enforced with meaningful penalties for infringement.

- ■ **Extent to which value is clearly planned with measurable objectives** This relates to the CSF concerning the approach to implementation, but reflects the fact that planning itself can vary in quality.

- ■ **Extent to which results are clearly communicated** ITAM needs good communication skills, but unfortunately these are not well developed by the career path for many ITAM practitioners.

- ■ **Extent to which silos are broken down** ITAM is most successful when it works in an integrated way with other functions (see also section 8.5).

- ■ **Extent of focus on sustainability** An appropriate focus must be placed on the sustainability of an ITAM programme to ensure its survival once early cost savings have been realized (see section 7.7).

Coping with decentralization

Many SAM/ITAM practitioners will have to operate in a decentralized organizational environment. Here are some suggestions for coping:

- ■ **Find out and leverage what is centralized** There are probably a number of corporate-level policies which do apply throughout the organization, even if largely ignored by local management. You may discover, for example, policies on good corporate governance or licence compliance that you can use to your advantage. The corporate annual report may give information about this level of policy.

- ■ **Find out about and coordinate with surrogate central ITAM management** There are probably other units with which you can work. For example, a corporate IT department which does not have authority over subsidiaries may still support common ITAM approaches and coordination.

- ■ **Find out about and coordinate with other ITAM functions** Discover what other units are doing relevant to ITAM and look for congruence. For example, you may be able to agree common tools, policies and procedures with other units that have similar infrastructures. It may also be possible to use consolidated purchasing arrangements, and even transfer unused licences between units.

- ■ **Be transparent with your local management** Enable them to see the benefits of what you are doing. Do not act in a way which makes them feel threatened.

In short, do everything you can to achieve the benefits of centralization without the structures of centralization. It will be a challenge, but the rewards will be worth it.

7.5.3 Critical failure factors

There are two factors which are most associated with the failure of ITAM projects, even if the CSFs described in section 7.5.1 are met. We refer to these as critical failure factors (CFFs):

- **Viewing a tool as a panacea** The most visible elements in the ITAM ecosystem are the tools promoted by ITAM tool vendors, which are discussed in Chapter 11. These are critical components of any successful ITAM implementation. However, they do not provide magic remedies. Good ITAM requires balanced focus on tools (i.e. products), people, processes and policy; and also on the discipline needed to ensure that all these function as intended. Many organizations have ITAM tools they have purchased in the past which have not been successfully exploited because the resources needed were not recognized or made available, or the required actions were not undertaken.

- **Insufficient licensing expertise** Given the importance of software licence compliance for most organizations, it is unfortunate to find that there is often insufficient licensing expertise applied to it. The complexity of software licensing affects both large and small organizations (but small organizations disproportionately), which has resulted in the significant growth of licensing advice being provided by external partners (see section 8.4).

7.5.4 Other challenges in achieving value

There are many detailed challenges for an ITAM project to deliver value in addition to the generic issues identified above as CSFs, VSFs and CFFs. These include the following:

- **Reconciliation with financial systems** The credibility of ITAM data is strengthened if it is reconciled with financial systems, but there are some major challenges and constraints in achieving this:
  - Much expenditure for IT assets is considered an expense for financial reporting purposes, and therefore there is no simple way to reconcile assets as defined for financial reporting purposes with those defined for ITAM purposes. Furthermore, the latter may not be eligible to be shown as assets in the financial books (e.g. leased equipment; cloud-based infrastructure and services; and employee-owned mobile devices).
  - Some expenditure cannot readily be classified in the financial books in a way which will easily reconcile with the way ITAM assets are defined. For example, some mainframe billings include both hardware and associated software, without a breakdown between the components.
  - To facilitate reconciling what can be reconciled, it is recommended that ITAM systems show, for all IT assets, who the legal owner is (in addition to who is the individual physically in charge of it). For any cost figures, data should also be provided to show the financial account against which that figure was recorded, and the date, plus any additional references needed to link the figure to the financial records.

- **Non-availability of some software licences needed** To correct possible underlicensing or to cover organizational growth, licences may be needed which are not available to purchase. For example, newer versions may have been released by the publisher, and downgrade rights may not be offered. Likewise, the publisher may have discontinued the software or the publisher may have gone out of business. It will generally require the organization to find an alternative to the software being used.

■ **Obtaining cost values for software assets** For calculating metrics on underlicensing, and potentially for determining the threshold value at which penalty pricing kicks in for some publisher licensing audits, it is necessary to know the costs of software assets (historical and/or current). Some issues may arise:

● Some historical cost data may not be available (e.g. old invoice records may have been destroyed or lost, such as in a merger).

● There may be difficulty allocating total invoice amounts to individual assets (as mentioned above for some mainframe billings).

It will be impossible in most situations to have fully accurate data, and indeed, it would be foolish to strive for excessive accuracy in this data which is meant for metrics and overall management control. Rather, it is suggested that the latest actual cost figure is used where possible and, failing that, a reasonable estimate.

7.6 COMMUNICATING VALUE

ITAM must market the value it delivers. There is an expression that the world won't beat a path to your door just because you build a better mousetrap. Likewise, the organization will not see the value delivered by ITAM if that value is not real, and if that value is not sold.

The manner by which SAM/ITAM is communicated to the business is often half the battle in convincing the business why it is needed. SAM/ITAM is necessary not just at the point of reporting on a software publisher audit but also in day-to-day IT operations.

Many non-IT people will lose interest in core counts, processor types, physical and virtual installs, etc., but a language they will understand is that of expense. If reports are presented showing consequential financial outlay for deploying software the wrong way, or highlighting cost savings measures for practising SAM/ITAM the right way, then they will gain the attention of the business.

While advice on selling is not the focus of this guide, a few suggestions may be useful:

■ **Be highly factual with your marketing** Highlight cost savings, metric improvements and other accomplishments. Quote others if appropriate.

■ **Be succinct** One paragraph of text should be enough to communicate your main message. A graphic or two can add impact.

■ **Do not undermine other units, and do not undermine your manager with your marketing** Rather, give your manager the credit for enabling your achievements.

7.7 SUSTAINING VALUE

Sustainability for SAM/ITAM in practical terms means being able to maintain a thriving ITAM programme beyond 3 years. Such a period is typically the time by which most easily made savings have been achieved and there have been no significantly adverse publisher audit findings to keep management's attention. Consequently, the 3-year mark is a typical one for ITAM programmes to be axed or severely curtailed.

There are two CSFs for achieving sustainability: (a) being seen to deliver continuing value to the organization; and (b) being indispensable for others to perform their jobs.

While the first of these is theoretically the more important, it is actually the second that is vital. This is because someone who is needed will be defended by others, whereas someone who just looks good on paper will probably not have that support. ITAM practices need to become an integral part of the culture of the organization. Both CSFs are discussed in more detail below:

■ **Being seen to deliver continuing value** This can be achieved in many ways, but the main requirement is to have good data to demonstrate the value being delivered. Some of the ways this can be achieved are:

- producing and maintaining cost-savings information. Savings identified during the current year/period should be highlighted. Historical savings information (e.g. terminated software maintenance costs) should also continue to be identified (see section 6.2).
- producing and maintaining key performance metrics (see section 7.3).
- ensuring that there are clear plans for ITAM activity (yearly at least, and by project where appropriate) with clear and measurable objectives, and reporting afterwards on results.

■ **Being indispensable to others** This ultimately comes down to attitude, although resourcing is also an issue. If the ITAM team operates in isolation, rebuffing requests for help from others, it cannot expect longer-term support. There may be a balancing act to perform between resource availability and the demands on those resources. This is one of the most important 'political' dimensions of the ITAM role and where management support becomes important: from the management of requesters

and from the management above ITAM. Some of the ways in which the ITAM role can become indispensable to others are:

- participating in key committees where ITAM advice can be critical, such as the change management or application release committees, the project management board, and other bodies performing similar functions, however named.
- supporting finance operationally by helping to review invoices for IT billings, particularly for those related to cloud services. Assistance can also be given in determining intra-company transfer billing/charging.
- supporting procurement strategically by understanding the alternative procurement arrangements available and their implications, and possibly by assisting in the process. For example, in a decentralized organization, ITAM could identify procurement arrangements of affiliates which could be utilized to achieve better pricing.
- supporting IT strategic planning, and project management, by providing expertise to minimize licensing costs. For example, ITAM can assist project managers by supplying licensing costings for scenario analyses; and, by using knowledge about products, can support application managers with their decisions relating to the application roadmap.
- supporting IT procurement operationally by being part of the procurement approval process.
- supporting IT deployment operationally by being part of the deployment approval process.

- supporting IT operations, and management overall, by providing data and reports which help them perform their jobs. (This is a common area for a conflict between available resources and the level of requests. Solutions need to be found, both short-term and long-term, to prevent support for ITAM being undermined.)
- supporting IT operations by managing much or all of the DML, which is simply the 'library' of resources needed by different parts of IT. Examples of resources which ITAM can manage include media, licence keys, stores of hardware and accessories, and contracts.

- supporting IT by providing ad-hoc advice on anything relating to ITAM, and in particular to software licensing. For example, ITAM should be able to advise on the licensing implications of infrastructure changes such as adding cores to a server.
- taking the initiative in understanding emerging issues for ITAM and in proposing solutions for the organizations. Examples of issues include MDM, the discovery and control of cloud services, and security (see also Chapter 4).

See also section 8.5.

People: leadership, organization, roles and responsibilities

8 People: leadership, organization, roles and responsibilities

8.1 THE CHANGING LANDSCAPE

As the world of IT continues to expand at a rapid pace, increasing demands are placed on SAM/ITAM which necessitate a concomitant evolution in how it is organized. Of course, how any organization structures itself, and the relevant roles and responsibilities for SAM/ITAM, are typically subject to management philosophy and 'politics'. Nonetheless, some basic guiding principles apply, and this chapter should be read in that context.

8.2 LEADERSHIP

Top-level leadership and an understanding of the role of SAM/ITAM are critical for the success of SAM/ITAM.

It is easy to state this requirement, but difficult to clarify quantitatively or qualitatively exactly what it means. It is perhaps easiest to explain in a negative way, with the observation that most failed or terminated SAM or ITAM programmes have not had the necessary top-level leadership.

Empirically, the following are common characteristics of organizations which demonstrate the right type of top-level leadership for successful SAM/ITAM:

■ The organization has a culture of good corporate governance. For public companies, this is typically reflected at a minimum in its annual report. Any organization with a culture of good corporate governance almost certainly has a clearly stated policy of compliance with all laws, regulations and contractual obligations.

■ The organization has a culture of operational excellence, in contrast to a culture of 'good enough'. Data in operational systems is expected to be accurate and reliable.

■ Accountability and empowerment for performance and compliance are given to individuals, not to groups such as the board in general.

There needs to be a named individual at a senior management level who actively takes ownership of the SAM/ITAM mission, and provides the necessary support to ensure its success. This person might, for example, be the CIO, chief financial officer (CFO) or the chief compliance officer.

The main issue is how the SAM/ITAM mission is defined and understood. The most common understanding of its mission is to achieve licence compliance such that there are no unexpected surprises in terms of budget hits, disruptions to other IT projects, or embarrassing publicity.

A more extensive mission statement for SAM/ITAM is also desirable and justified. Such a mission statement might be 'to drive business value by meeting the organization's IT asset requirements in a responsive and cost-effective way, integrated with IT security and logistical requirements'.

8.3 WHERE SAM/ITAM SHOULD REPORT

The primary responsibility for SAM/ITAM can reside in multiple places within the organization; each has its own considerations, both positive and negative. Table 8.1 provides some examples.

8.4 CONSIDERATIONS ABOUT OUTSOURCING AND MANAGED SERVICES

One of the major trends to emerge in IT has been the use of outsourcing (which is the term used for relatively large groupings of activities performed by external organizations) and managed services (more limited services performed by external organizations). SAM/ITAM may be outsourced as part of a larger IT outsourcing deal, or contracted out as managed services separate from the remainder of IT activity.

One major warning applies for all outsourcing and managed services: while activities can be outsourced, the associated risks and exposures generally cannot be contracted away. For example, the exposure to licence compliance audits generally falls into this category. Consequently, it is essential that the organization retains an in-house risk-monitoring function, even for outsourced activities and managed services.

This being said, there are major benefits to be achieved with SAM/ITAM, reflected in the significant uptake of such managed services in recent years. Indeed, Gartner (2015) predicted the following:

■ By 2018, the SAM skills shortage would make 50 per cent of organizations (who had implemented or were in the process of implementing SAM) dependent on managed SAM services.

Table 8.1 Where SAM/ITAM should report

Organizational reporting under	Considerations
CIO	Helps secure IT executive sponsorship for SAM/ITAM but may be removed from the other stakeholders and from daily IT operations
IT operations	Good integration with IT processes and access to IT systems and resources but may be too removed from the legal/procurement and finance stakeholders
Procurement and vendor management	Best integration with daily vendor management activities, contract negotiations etc. Typically, would result in good integration with finance department but limited integration with IT
CFO	More neutral location, and may help ensure financial focus/discipline to the work done, but typically is too removed from the other stakeholders, resulting in limited integration with IT
Security management	Good integration with security and risk activities. Not yet practised widely enough to know its limitations
Internal audit/risk management	More neutral location; however, tends to lack focus on optimization objectives, typically resulting in limited integration with IT

■ By 2017, enterprises would spend ten times more on SAM services than they were spending on SAM tools.

SAM as a Service (SAMaaS) (or ITAM as a Service (ITAMaaS)) is an emerging best practice adopted by an increasing number of organizations who come to the realization that (a) effective SAM/ITAM is a key business objective, and (b) software licensing is not a core competency of the organization (and more importantly, should not be).

Some of the pros for SAMaaS may include:

■ **Access to the best industry talent** This is becoming more critical with the increasing competition for good talent in the market

■ **Access to best industry practices** Avoid mistakes, leverage what has been implemented successfully at hundreds of other organizations, etc.

■ **Ability to increase SAM/ITAM resources/capacity as needed** For example, use more consultants during an implementation or an audit defence exercise, and fewer at other times

■ **Access to specialists** Understanding the licensing nuances of the large software publishers often requires a singular focus (i.e. an individual who dedicates years to focus on just one publisher). On the other hand, even the largest end-user organizations do not require a dedicated full-time-equivalent employee for each publisher. (As an aside, even Fortune 50 companies often only require a few weeks every year of deep Microsoft or Oracle licensing expertise). Instead of recruiting expensive full-time specialists, the organization acquires the help of appropriate experts for only the period when it needs them.

Note that there are many possible variants of SAMaaS. One of these is simply to engage a third-party organization with specialist licensing expertise to provide regular and also on-demand services. The other end of the spectrum involves having the third-party organization provide the necessary SAM/ITAM tools and have operational responsibility for them. Be careful that the tools themselves are properly licensed (e.g. if run on the third party's database servers). See also Appendix G.

8.5 DEALING WITH SILOS

There appears to be a natural tendency for organizations to work in functional isolation ('silos') as they get larger. For the purposes of SAM/ITAM, the most common major silos are the following:

■ **Procurement** This may operate with significant autonomy from the IT department. The risk is that it may be more concerned with immediate visible savings than with the longer-term support and cost implications of procurement decisions (see also section 8.6).

■ **Service management** Since SAM/ITAM is not covered in detail in the core ITIL publications, the risk is that ITSM personnel may not see a significant reason for working together. In particular, if SAM /ITAM is seen as only concerned with licence compliance, it may not be considered an issue for ITSM.

■ **Security** Traditionally, security and SAM/ITAM typically have not worked together to any significant degree. They should, however, be highly integrated, and there is some sign of movement in this direction (see Chapter 14).

■ **Infrastructure support and development teams** Many organizations have separate infrastructure teams for different technologies and applications. These teams frequently have different working practices and methods, particularly when it comes to the management of assets.

■ **Project management** IT projects are generally one of the largest consumers of SAM/ITAM expertise. Project managers, being responsible for acquiring software, need the active help of SAM/ITAM to support them in their selection of licensing models.

■ **SAM/ITAM** SAM/ITAM tends to work in comparative isolation, with their primary reason for existence being seen as licence compliance (which may be viewed in a negative light), rather than as a business enabler.

Empirically, the following have been observed to facilitate the breaking down of these silos:

■ **Membership of the change advisory board (CAB) or equivalent** Having representatives of different silos on a change control committee appears to be one of the most effective ways of ensuring they work together effectively. SAM/ITAM and security in particular should be included, to ensure that licensing and security issues are considered in the decisions taken.

■ **Membership of the boards for the approval of applications and projects** SAM/ITAM and security need to support application and project management to ensure that licensing and security issues are considered in the decisions taken.

■ **Common management tool architecture and use of common tools and databases** The tool provider community is one of the best drivers for cooperation between different silos, because good data provided by any one silo will typically be highly useful to the others. The definition, agreement and implementation of a management tool architecture or the integration of management tools can act as a great driver for collaboration and interworking between silos (see Chapter 11).

■ **Consolidated corporate policies** Each of the silos has requirements which ideally should be covered by corporate policies. Many of these requirements are complementary or may even overlap. Developing corporate policies which consolidate these separate requirements will encourage joint working and cooperation between the silos (note that the corporate policies should not be overly detailed; see Chapter 9).

■ **Common reporting lines** Multiple functions reporting to the same manager, without significant disparity in either size or influence, can be a strong driver for better cooperation between those functions. For example, in a few organizations security and ITAM are starting to report to the same manager, which facilitates cooperative working.

■ **Knowledge-sharing** The creation of a knowledge management process and encouragement of knowledge-sharing within all areas will improve the quality and accuracy of management data areas across the organization.

■ **Integrated management system** The establishment of a single integrated management system across all IT processes and activities can act as a real catalyst for breaking down barriers and silos and for increasing integration and collaboration. This means the integration, in particular, of the management systems for IT service management (ISO/IEC 20000-1), information security management (ISO/IEC 27001) and IT asset management (ISO/IEC 19770-1).

8.6 RESPECTIVE ROLES OF PROCUREMENT MANAGEMENT AND IT MANAGEMENT

Another important decision to be made concerns the respective roles of procurement management and IT management. Responsibility for IT procurement typically is defined in one of two ways:

■ The department responsible for procurement (often called 'procurement', 'purchasing' or 'supply chain') has principal responsibility for managing all aspects of IT procurement, with guidance to the extent necessary from IT management and personnel.

■ The department responsible for IT has principal responsibility for managing all aspects of IT procurement, with guidance to the extent necessary from procurement department personnel.

Key message

On balance, assuming typical skill profiles, it is better to give the primary responsibility for IT procurement to the IT department, but with a strong supporting role being played by procurement. If strategic procurement functions are centralized as described in section 7.5.2, it will be easier to ensure sufficient qualified resources are dedicated to the job from both areas.

Reasons for giving principal responsibility to the department responsible for procurement include:

■ It is unlikely to be swayed by the idea of technology for its own sake, and therefore better placed to take cold economic decisions about the cost justification of proposed expenditure.

■ It is better prepared to deal with the legal paperwork of contracting.

■ It has better negotiating skills, and can drive a harder bargain.

■ It may have capacity to perform the work, compared with a possibly overworked IT department.

Reasons for giving principal responsibility to the IT department include:

■ IT personnel have to live with the day-to-day consequences of procurement decisions, and they will be more acutely focused on the operational implications of contracts and what is necessary to meet contractual obligations.

■ IT personnel may also give more attention to other non-quantifiable factors, such as the audit reputation of a publisher.

■ IT personnel have a better view on strategic IT directions and alternatives, which is where some of the most significant savings can be identified.

■ IT personnel may have more of a 'risk management' orientation because of related concerns in areas such as security and data protection.

8.7 ROLES AND RESPONSIBILITIES

If SAM/ITAM processes are to prove successful within an organization, it is important that roles and responsibilities are clearly defined and agreed, together with the scope of ownership of each of the processes. These roles and responsibilities should therefore be adapted to fit the individual requirements of each organization in accordance with its size, nature, structure, culture and geographical distribution. In small organizations, one or two people will perform most of these roles; some roles may also be outsourced, or provided as a managed service (see section 8.4).

Table 8.2 RACI for software licence reconciliations

Activity	SAM/ITAM process owner	Software licensing specialist	Contract lifecycle operations specialist	Licence entitlement specialist	Licence reconciliation specialist	Licence consumption specialist	Compliance remediation owner	Demand manager	Operations manager	Contracts and commercial specialist
Calculate entitlement position										
Manual loading of proof of licence	A		C	R						
Entitlement analysis: automated	A			R						
Entitlement analysis: manual	A	C		R						
Record entitlement results	A	I	I	R						
Calculate consumption position										
Consumption analysis: automated	A					R				
Consumption analysis: manual	A	C				R				
Calculate reconciliation position										
Reconciliation analysis	A				R					
Extract auto-reconciliation data	A				R					
Perform nuanced analysis	A	C			R					
Perform nuanced reconciliation	A	C			R					
Record nuanced reconciliation	A	I	I		R					
Compliance reporting										
Run automated reports	A				R					
Run ad-hoc reports	A				R					
Validate/QA reports	A	C			R					
Distribute reports: internal	A		C		R					

Activity	SAM/ITAM process owner	Software licensing specialist	Contract lifecycle operations specialist	Licence entitlement specialist	Licence reconciliation specialist	Licence consumption specialist	Compliance remediation owner	Demand manager	Operations manager	Contracts and commercial specialist
Compliance reporting *continued*										
File reports	A				R					
Distribute reports to publisher			I							A, R
Support validation					C				A, R	
Remediation planning										
Analysis of reconciliation results	A	R					C			I
Calculate optimal remediation approach	A	R					C	C		I

R = responsible; A = accountable; C = consulted; I = informed

Table 8.2 gives a RACI analysis (identifying each responsibility as either responsible, accountable, consulted or informed) of some of the main roles and responsibilities within the SAM/ITAM function.

8.7.1 Primary roles

A number of roles need to be considered when establishing SAM/ITAM practices. It must be stressed that these are roles rather than positions or full-time jobs within an organization, so they will often be shared between or assigned to personnel who also have other roles and responsibilities. The primary SAM/ITAM roles that need to be considered are:

- **Management sponsor** It is important if SAM/ITAM is to succeed within an organization that sponsorship and commitment are obtained from senior management, both within the business as a whole and within the IT department. This will ensure that: (a) the visibility of SAM/ITAM is maintained, (b) the organizational culture is developed to enable SAM/ITAM processes to succeed, and (c) sufficient budget and resources will be obtained. Such management sponsorship and commitment must not be allowed to deteriorate (see also section 8.2).

- **Service asset manager/configuration manager** This role has overall responsibility for service asset and configuration management, as defined in ITIL. In an ITIL-conformant organization, those responsible for SAM/ITAM might report to the configuration manager, although as defined here it would mean an expansion of the role of service asset and configuration management.

■ **SAM/ITAM process owner and manager** In some organizations, responsibility for the overall effectiveness and efficiency of SAM/ITAM processes rests with the process owner. The process manager is responsible for the day-to-day operation of SAM/ITAM and the process owner is accountable for the process, its improvement and its high-level objectives.

■ **IT asset manager** This role should be responsible for the management of all IT assets within an organization and have overall responsibility for establishing and maintaining the IT asset database (this is technically part of the CMS in ITIL terminology; see Chapter 11). The database should contain all the information required by SAM/ITAM processes. Often, this asset management responsibility is distributed within the individual technical support teams (e.g. the server team manages the server assets and asset register).

■ **Software asset manager** This is the role with responsibility for the management of all software assets within an organization, which is a subset of the IT asset manager's overall responsibility. If the responsibilities are separated (they are often merged), it is essential that common processes and a common database are shared between the two roles.
See also section 1.4.

8.7.2 Primary sub-roles (within the SAM/ITAM function)

Many sub-roles also need to be considered when establishing SAM/ITAM practices; again, these can either be completed by a single person or be combined with one or more of the primary roles. The primary SAM/ITAM sub-roles that need to be considered are:

■ **Software licensing specialist** Licensing specialists (who focus on both the licensing rules and the entitlement and deployment analysis of one or more of the organization's software publishers, such as Microsoft, IBM, and Oracle) are key to an effective SAM/ITAM programme. If you only have SAM/ITAM generalists (who can implement and manage best-practice SAM processes), you may accumulate plenty of good data but nobody will be in a position to interpret it and take meaningful action. The concept of deep publisher-by-publisher expertise is the critical 'last mile' which many companies fail to complete (even those few that otherwise do have effective SAM/ITAM). Software licensing specialists are often from outside the organization. If the organization has separately designated personnel for the specialist roles relating to entitlement, reconciliation and consumption, then the software licensing specialist acts as quality control for their work.

■ **Licence entitlement specialist** This role involves recording all licence entitlements and performing necessary calculations (upgrades, maintenance etc.) to determine the licence entitlements positions available to be used. (In smaller organizations, this role may be combined with the next two.)

■ **Licence consumption specialist** The holder of this role is responsible for determining the consumption of (i.e. usage against) licence entitlements. The measurement of consumption can be highly specific to a particular software publisher, licensing model, software and even hardware, so specialist knowledge and even specialist software or hardware may be required. (In smaller organizations, this role may be combined with the next one.)

- **Licence reconciliation specialist** The holder of this role is responsible for reconciling licence entitlements with licence consumption. They may require specialist licensing knowledge, because the entitlements and the consumption may not be for equivalent products or quantities. For example, entitlements may include both downgrade and upgrade rights, which need to be understood correctly to perform the reconciliation accurately.
- **Compliance remediation owner** The holder of this role must be consulted about any compliance remediation actions which are required on the basis of the licence reconciliation reports. This role may have the budgetary responsibility for any underlicensing identified.
- **Demand manager** The role holder is responsible for managing total consumption of (specific) software products within the organization. In the case of remediation actions needed to address underlicensing identified by licence reconciliations, they may consider solutions which reduce demand (e.g. by uninstalling software which is effectively unused). This role also involves responsibility for 'licence optimization', also known as 'licence harvesting'.
- **Contract lifecycle operations specialist** The person in this role is responsible for remediating any underlicensing identified by licence reconciliations, after consulting with the demand manager and the compliance remediation owner.
- **Contracts and commercial specialist** The holder of this role is responsible for liaising with software publishers or resellers, and with the provision of consumption and licence reconciliation reports where contractually obligated.

- **Asset analyst or configuration librarian** This role has responsibility for maintaining up-to-date (and historical) records of IT assets, including software version control.
- **SAM/ITAM management tool analyst or automation analyst** This analyst is responsible for the implementation, configuring and tailoring of tools to automate processes wherever it is cost-effective.
- **SAM/ITAM consultant** The SAM/ITAM consultant is usually from outside the organization and provides advice and guidance on all aspects of SAM/ITAM best practice.

8.7.3 Complementary roles

There are also many roles in other areas whose involvement in SAM/ITAM activities is critical to their success. Some of the principal complementary SAM/ITAM roles in other areas are:

- **Security manager** This role is not strictly a SAM/ITAM role but it has a crucial part to play in the operation of effective SAM/ITAM processes. The security manager should help ensure that all software is maintained at the recommended security 'patch level' so that security exposures from the use of software are minimized. This role also has significant responsibilities with regard to assets: asset protection; risk assessment, management and mitigation; and security classification.
- **Human resources** HR can provide assistance where policy breaches are detected or there is misuse of organizational assets.
- **Service desk manager** Although this role is not strictly a SAM/ITAM role, it is a vital one. The service desk manager has a responsibility to ensure that all contacts with the service desk

that uncover instances of unauthorized or unapproved software are reported to the SAM/ITAM exception processes as soon as possible for review and resolution.

■ **Operations manager** Although primarily responsible for server-side operations, this role also includes responsibility for helping to validate software licence compliance reports.

■ **Procurement management** Personnel in this area are responsible for all aspects of the procurement process within the end-user organization.

■ **Change manager** The change manager ensures that an effective change management process is in place to control all changes within the IT infrastructure, including those to software.

■ **Release and deployment manager** This role involves ensuring that only authentic licensed software is deployed to approved destinations, and reviewed and audited on completion.

■ **Auditors (internal and external)** These are responsible for reviewing and auditing the SAM/ITAM processes for efficiency, effectiveness and compliance.

■ **Legal adviser** Responsible for the provision of legal advice and guidance on contractual issues; the role may be filled in-house but this is less likely in smaller organizations.

Policy

9

9 Policy

ITAM policies will typically be defined at multiple levels, from the highest organizational level to that of acceptable use policies relevant to individual end-users. Some relevant observations are:

- Policies are strongest and most effective if they are established at the top organizational level, but they are also generally the least detailed here, tending to be statements of principle (e.g. of good corporate governance including compliance with all relevant legislation, regulation and contractual terms and conditions).

- It is desirable to establish consolidated policies at the highest organizational level for multiple areas (e.g. ITAM, IT security, IT procurement and personal data protection). This is a strong mechanism to drive better coordination and cooperation between different areas, in preference to each having its own unique policies which may be inconsistently disseminated and enforced.

- Lower-level policies (e.g. by subsidiary, business unit or function, such as procurement) will generally be more detailed, and may also specify procedures. The acceptable use policy is one specific example. It applies to all end-users throughout the organization, and generally needs to be explicitly acknowledged by each end-user to help ensure understanding and compliance, as well as to avoid legal issues for the organization in the event of an individual's non-compliance.

ITAM policies will typically cover the following, at varying degrees of detail depending on the level in the organization at which they are defined:

- roles and responsibilities for ITAM
- policies and procedures for the procurement of IT assets
- standard/preferred products, architectures, publishers and resellers
- policies and procedures for the distribution and installation of IT assets
- policies and procedures for the retirement of IT assets.

The acceptable use policy may cover the following:

- General responsibilities of the individual:
  - to respect the assets of the organization, including its reputation, intellectual property, data, hardware and software, and to take all reasonable steps to protect them
  - to comply with all relevant legislation, regulations and contractual commitments of the organization, including for software licence compliance
  - to make all reasonable efforts to know and understand the organization's policies and procedures (related to IT assets), and to comply with them.
- Purposes for which the organization's IT assets may be used by the individual:
  - business purposes
  - limited personal use with clarification as to what this permits (which may be defined separately, subject to change, such as limited use of email as long as it will not be interpreted as representing the organization; possible limited use of social media).

- Purposes for which the organization's IT assets may not be used by the individual:
  - performing any illegal or inappropriate activity (e.g. accessing or storing content such as pornography)
  - personal business activity.
- Restrictions on what the individual is not allowed to do without explicit authorization:
  - copying the organization's data or software for personal use, or to supply to third parties
  - copying software for additional installations
  - purchasing or installing software which has not been pre-approved in accordance with the organization's policies, including in particular software downloaded from the internet
  - contracting for IT services which have not been pre-approved in accordance with the organization's policies, including in particular for cloud services.
- Purposes for which the organization may maintain personal data, monitor individuals, or use data about individuals:
  - monitoring usage of the organization's IT assets including the organization's data (e.g. monitoring the use of software to facilitate licence harvesting; and monitoring data transfers to identify possibly unauthorized data exfiltration)
  - monitoring an individual's personal hardware, software or data which has any connection to the organization's facilities/IT assets (e.g. monitoring software and data on any devices used by an individual that are connected to the organization's systems, including emails and social messaging)
  - maintaining data about an individual for management and operational purposes (to avoid issues associated with data protection legislation in some jurisdictions).
- Consequences of failure to comply with these policies:
  - disciplinary action as stated within the organization's employee handbook
  - civil or criminal proceedings where appropriate.
- Acknowledgement (in writing or by other method that can be authenticated) by each individual that they understand and agree to these policies.

Processes 10

10 Processes

10.1 PROCESS OVERVIEW

There are three process areas within SAM/ITAM, as introduced in section 1.5 and illustrated in Figure 1.2. This chapter describes each of these process areas in more detail:

■ management system processes for ITAM
■ functional management processes for IT assets
■ lifecycle management processes for IT assets.

Too often areas of SAM/ITAM are implemented within their own discrete areas, isolated (for example) from the server-side infrastructure and other ITSM processes. It is, however, essential that the SAM/ITAM processes and activities are seen to be an integral part of all other IT management systems and processes; in other words, that they work together as a single integrated management system.

10.2 MANAGEMENT SYSTEM PROCESSES FOR ITAM

There are seven overarching management system processes within the ITAMS, as shown in Figure 10.1.

These processes provide governance and management of the ITAMS and ITAM activities and can briefly be described as follows.

10.2.1 Governance

Two process areas provide direction and control of ITAM practices:

■ **Understanding the external context and stakeholder needs** The organization must understand the internal and external issues affecting ITAMS, and also the stakeholder needs and expectations. This process is the driver for all the other processes.

■ **Leadership, policy and organization** This process has both a governance and a management component. The governance aspect involves converting the knowledge about the external context and stakeholder needs into high-level policy and objectives.

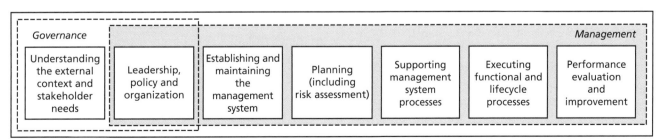

Figure 10.1 The management system processes for ITAM

10.2.2 Management

The following six process areas provide the management activities required to satisfy the governance needs:

- **Leadership, policy and organization** The management aspect of this process takes the high-level policy and objectives established at the governance level and translates them into the mid-level policies, objectives and organization needed to fulfil them.

- **Establishing and maintaining the management system** This process entails defining the scope of the ITAMS and then implementing and maintaining it. Note that the ITAMS is much more than simply computer systems; it includes all the processes and activities required, including areas such as training.

- **Planning (including risk assessment)** A major part of the planning process concerns risk assessment and the associated subject of risk treatment (e.g. mitigation measures). It also includes the determination of detailed ITAM objectives. For ISO SAM/ITAM, this is where the 'tier' and the corresponding detailed objectives for the ITAMS will be determined (see section C.2).

- **Supporting management system processes** This process ensures that the resources required to plan, establish, operate and improve the ITAMS are available and coordinated, and that the personnel involved have the required capabilities and competences. It also makes sure that those concerned are aware of ITAM policies, plans and objectives and are provided with the appropriate communication, documentation and information. Another function is to determine the information and audit trail requirements for ITAM; although these are up-front activities, they require periodic revisiting.

- **Executing functional and lifecycle management processes** This provides the link between ITAM as an overall system and the management of IT assets themselves. It is the higher-level process to ensure that all functional and lifecycle activities are planned, executed and controlled to meet the desired objectives.

- **Performance evaluation and improvement** This process ensures that the performance of the ITAMS and its processes and activities are continually monitored and measured. Following the completion of regular (planned) management reviews and audits, corrective and proactive preventative actions should be taken to address identified weaknesses, failures and potential issues. This ensures that no matter how mature or effective ITAM processes are, appropriate opportunities for improvement are continually pursued.

10.3 FUNCTIONAL MANAGEMENT PROCESSES FOR IT ASSETS

In SAM/ITAM, the functional processes are those which deal with specific issues relating to IT assets throughout their lifecycles, such as security.

The ITAM functional processes are shown in Figure 10.2 and discussed in the following sub-sections. Most of these process areas correspond to ITIL processes, with the exception of licence management. Consequently, for most processes reference will be made to the relevant processes from the ITIL core publications, with comments added for particular SAM/ITAM concerns.

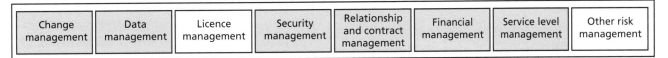

Figure 10.2 The functional management processes for IT assets

Note: The shaded boxes are those processes which are already significantly covered in the ITIL core publications.

10.3.1 Change management

Purpose
To control all changes throughout the asset lifecycle, enabling beneficial changes to be made with minimum disruption to IT services.

The change management process for SAM/ITAM is essentially the same as that for ITSM as described in *ITIL Service Transition* (2011). Reference should be made there for detailed guidance.

Change management can be triggered in different ways (see section 10.4.2 for a description of the main ones for SAM/ITAM; namely service requests, change requests and business initiatives).

10.3.2 Data management

Purpose
To ensure that required data is collected and accurately recorded for all IT assets, throughout their lifecycles.

The data management process for SAM/ITAM is essentially the same as the service asset and configuration management process for ITSM in *ITIL Service Transition*. Reference should be made there for detailed guidance.

The data management process excludes licensing data and related calculations, which are covered by the licence management process (see section 10.3.3). The data management and licence management processes are separated because (a) the data management process is more closely aligned with the ITIL service asset and configuration management process as often actually implemented by ITSM, and (b) the licence management process goes far beyond anything which is specified in ITIL, and indeed is the most distinguishing process of SAM/ITAM. To subsume something so complex into another more generic process would be to diminish its criticality in SAM/ITAM, and to the organization as a whole, especially for the purposes of achieving licence compliance.

The data management process includes data verification, which is exceptionally important for SAM/ITAM. Indeed, Tier 1 in ISO ITAM (ISO/IEC 19770-1 IT asset management) is called 'trustworthy data' in recognition of the importance of complete and accurate data. ISO ITAM requires that quantitative targets are set for data accuracy, and this is highly recommended for any organization implementing SAM/ITAM processes.

Key message
Too many organizations have assumed that installing a SAM/ITAM tool is all they need to do to manage their IT assets, and to achieve software licence compliance. The 'GiGo' acronym (garbage in, garbage out) that was prevalent during the 1960s and 70s still holds true today. If data quality is not achieved for SAM/ITAM, then everything else which relies on it is at risk, including licence compliance and ITSM as a whole.

The data verification tests should consider:

- **Scope** Are all the assets deemed to be within the scope of the SAM/ITAM activities discovered and is the appropriate information gathered?
- **Asset use** Can the status/role of assets be determined (e.g. so that an organization does not have to pay the cost of production licences for development or training installations of software?)
- **Orphan data** Once data is in the ITAM tool, is it possible to resolve any orphan data that are not immediately linkable between installed assets, identified assets (e.g. using recognition files or engines) and entitlements (see also section 10.5)?
- **Archiving/disposal** Once a software title has been retired, is there a robust process by which supporting data is archived or removed?
- **Data reconciliation** Is the data regularly reconciled with other data and information repositories (e.g. accounting and financial management information), and are differences and variances resolved?

10.3.3 Licence management

Purpose

To ensure that the required data concerning licences, licence entitlements and licence usage is accurately recorded for all IT assets, throughout their lifecycles.

The licence management process covers licensing data and related calculations, and is the process which most visibly differentiates SAM/ITAM from ITSM as defined by ITIL. Licence management is not covered by the core ITIL publications.

In some respects licence management is similar to the data management process (see section 10.3.2) because it covers licensing data in a similar way to

how the data management covers data about non-licence assets. However, licence management goes beyond that. Overall, the licence management process covers the following:

- **Raw licensing data** This is data about specific licences, such as the product covered (including version); the characteristics of the licences (e.g. whether they are full, upgrade or maintenance; perpetual or subscription); their proposed usage (commercial, educational, governmental or personal); the procurement details (such as date of purchase; from whom; cost; quantity); and any other terms and conditions associated with the licence which are needed for licence management (e.g. transferability in some situations).
- **Entitlement information** 'Effective licensing' or entitlement information is the usage which is permitted by licences after all relevant factors have been taken into account. In principle this is calculated or analysed data, which at its simplest can be raw licensing data without any analysis (e.g. with perpetual licences for full products), and at its most complex can be challenging even for licensing experts to understand. Examples of the types of consideration which may need to be taken into account are:
  - What products are eligible for upgrades or combinations with what other products?
  - Which licence types are eligible to be used at all, or combined to produce further entitlements (e.g. whether original equipment manufacturer (OEM) licences, licences from affiliates, and/or transferred licences are eligible)?
  - If for maintenance, what upgrades came out during the period covered by the maintenance?
  - Are rights available for some licences in addition to those received with the original

purchase, such as variations allowing for use in cloud deployments, and technology guarantees?

- Are there other rights which attach to the entitlements, such as downgrade rights and conversion rights to alternative entitlements (e.g. types of CAL)?

- How will usage against the entitlement be measured?

■ **Usage data** Usage against an entitlement is measured data, but the measurement may be complex. At its simplest it can based on the number of installed instances of software, but even these situations are somewhat rare now given the prevalence of secondary installation rights, and the trend to license cloud use over multiple devices per person. Violation of licensing terms and conditions by sharing user IDs can also result in incorrect usage measurements and licensing shortfalls. Some of the most challenging types of usage to measure (and costly in terms of licence non-compliance) are those based on access rights, with licensing terms and conditions dictating that any use of connector or concentrator-type technology can significantly expand what needs to be measured (and licensed) as compared with what IT personnel may expect. There are also major challenges in measuring processor usage for server products, which may vary significantly (with cost implications) as a result of unpredictable changes by (cloud) data centre personnel increasing server resources to maintain service levels, or moving virtual machines around in a way which creates major licensing exposures.

■ **Licence compliance calculations** Usage needs to be compared with entitlements to determine a licence compliance position. This can introduce yet more complexity in addition to that which already exists in determining entitlements and

usage against them. Often, especially for large organizations, there will be alternative ways of matching usage to entitlements (e.g. because there will be more than one entitlement which can cover a given usage owing to downgrade rights). The licence compliance position determined should be the one which works best for the organization. Usually this will be the one with the least underlicensing cost, but a more expensive alternative might be more strategic because of the options it creates.

Note that ITAM standards for software identification, entitlements and resource utilization measurement have all been developed to help address the complexities of the issues discussed above (see Appendix D for more information on these standards (ISO/IEC 19770-2, 3 and 4)).

In order to perform meaningful licence compliance calculations it is necessary to have meaningful costing information both (a) to assess the cost implications of any underlicensing identified, but also (b) for other management purposes (e.g. to demonstrate the investment in IT assets; to identify the savings from recycling; and to demonstrate the costs of alternative strategies going forward, such as changing products, architectures or publishers); see also section 10.3.6.

Total investment and yearly spend, especially in software (in total and by publisher), can be useful for establishing bands of likelihood as to possible underlicensing exposures. Some organizations budget contingency amounts based on these calculations so as to reduce the potential budgetary impact of licence compliance audits.

The licence management process includes data verification, and also verification of all calculations, including those relating to licence compliance.

Because of the extreme complexity of this area, it is highly recommended that independent licensing expertise be used as part of verification (see section 8.4 and Appendix G for more information).

Licensing expertise is needed not only in the licence management process but in many other processes. One of the most important is in the specification process (section 10.4.2), which includes 'licensing by design'.

10.3.4 Security management

Purpose

To ensure that SAM/ITAM processes and activities are compliant with all organizational security policies, processes and requirements.

The security management process for SAM/ITAM is essentially the same as the information security management process for ITSM as described in *ITIL Service Design* (2011). Reference should be made there for detailed guidance.

There are two aspects of security management that need to be addressed:

■ security internal to SAM/ITAM activities and processes
■ security external to SAM/ITAM practices in support of the larger information security mission and policy of the business.

Internal considerations should address access to source/deployment code and to the SAM/ITAM tool itself. Considering how a SAM/ITAM tool can act as a repository of some very powerful data (and also sensitive data personal to users), controlling access to it should be a fundamental security requirement for SAM/ITAM management. Activities and processes should also ensure that SAM/ITAM policies and processes are compliant with all security management policies and processes, and that all security patches are applied promptly to all relevant assets.

Wherever possible, SAM/ITAM activities and processes should assist security; there should be close collaboration and integration between SAM/ITAM and all security management processes and activities.

Managers should only release reports produced by the SAM/ITAM tool on a need-to-know basis, and should ensure that information requests are vetted prior to being satisfied. This also applies to publisher licence compliance audits, where only data that is necessary and does not potentially compromise the organization should be supplied. Information inappropriately supplied about users may breach data protection legislation. In addition, information about specific software and versions in use may create security issues if outsiders know it has exposures capable of being exploited.

Information security best practice seeks to create a citadel whose boundary is defined by an information security management system (ISMS). Undoubtedly, the IT estate forms a sizeable part of that boundary, so being able to confirm that certain users have access to particular databases (as an example) or that new devices have been added to the network, will prove invaluable to the information security team.

10.3.5 Relationship and contract management

Purpose

To ensure that customer relationships are managed to help achieve customer satisfaction; and that supplier relationships (both internal and external) are managed to ensure value for money and the seamless quality of IT services.

The relationship and contract management process for SAM/ITAM is essentially the combination of two separate processes in ITIL, namely the business relationship management process described in *ITIL Service Strategy* (2011) (covering customer-side relationships), and the supplier management process described in *ITIL Service Design* (covering supplier-side relationships). Reference should be made there for detailed guidance.

SAM/ITAM relationships with end-users are typically governed by an SLA between the IT department and end-user management. Consequently, SAM/ITAM practitioners need to coordinate with the IT department's business or customer relationship managers to ensure that issues relevant to SAM/ITAM are properly coordinated. It may also be appropriate to have OLAs with other units within the IT department (e.g. to define response times for information requests, and specify how issues relating to licensing will be coordinated); see also section 10.3.7.

SAM/ITAM practitioners are often closely involved in supplier relationships, and in some cases have significant procurement management responsibilities. When signing important new contracts and engaging with new suppliers, it is often worth seeking legal advice and guidance, either internally within the organization or from external legal experts. There are also many external SAM/ITAM organizations within this area that can offer specialist experience and advice.

10.3.6 Financial management

Purpose

To ensure that costs and returns associated with IT assets are properly monitored and managed.

The financial management process for SAM/ITAM is similar to the financial management for IT services process for ITSM as described in *ITIL Service Strategy*. Reference should be made there for detailed guidance.

SAM/ITAM financial management includes:

- ensuring the preparation of reliable financial information for all software and hardware assets throughout their lifecycles, including during their acquisition, operation (e.g. regular depreciation) and their subsequent retirement and disposal
- collecting cost-benefit information related to the use of hardware and software assets, to allow the calculation of TCO and the ROI
- ensuring that there is appropriate financial approval for all new software and hardware acquisitions
- ensuring proper consideration of accounting and tax practices and requirements.

The biggest exposure which senior management typically sees with respect to SAM/ITAM is the risk of major unexpected budgetary hits resulting from underlicensing identified by publisher audits. While better performance of the licence management function can reduce this exposure, a complementary approach used by some organizations is to establish a contingency for negative licence compliance findings (see section 10.3.3).

Relevant expertise should be used to ensure that accounting and tax treatments for software and hardware assets are appropriate and tax efficient. Depending on the country involved and other factors such as tax position and industry, significant savings may be possible through a combination of good record-keeping and proper application of the relevant tax regulations. Alternatively, inappropriate procurement in some countries (e.g. via global purchasing agreements not based in that country) can have significantly negative legal and financial implications.

As a SAM/ITAM practitioner, it would be good practice to understand the basics of financial reporting. In addition, gaining knowledge of financial practices such as TCO, ROI and the concept of depreciation will enable financially focused ITAM reports to be better understood by the business; and in particular by finance.

Regular financial reviews should be conducted of asset investments to ensure that costs are effectively managed and that contracts and suppliers are continually consolidated to the extent practicable.

10.3.7 Service level management

Purpose
To ensure that all current and planned services are delivered to agreed achievable service levels and targets.

The service level management (SLM) process for SAM/ITAM is essentially the same as service level management for ITSM in *ITIL Service Design*. SLM has a role to play in managing customer end-user expectations by discussing, defining and agreeing achievable targets and levels of performance within service level requirements (SLRs) and SLAs. SLAs and SLRs should include agreed targets for such activities as:

■ fulfilment of hardware and software requests
■ implementation of hardware and software changes
■ implementation of hardware and software moves
■ timescales and frequencies of hardware and software updates, releases and deployments.

SLM should also ensure that all customer and user roles and responsibilities are agreed and documented within SLAs. Documented responsibilities should include a requirement for all users of IT services and systems to accept, agree, sign and abide by the organization's policies on software, security, software usage and internet usage, before using and accessing IT services and systems. See also section 7.3.6.

10.3.8 Other risk management

Purpose
To manage all identified risks which are not managed by any other SAM/ITAM processes.

The 'other' risk management process for SAM/ITAM covers any identified risks which are not already covered elsewhere. The main such risks identified in ISO ITAM are for business continuity, as covered in the IT service continuity management process and in the availability management process described in *ITIL Service Design*. Reference should be made there for detailed guidance. Other risks which might also be addressed in this process are regulatory compliance risks (e.g. for specific industries and for specific legal requirements, such as for personal data protection legislation).

The management of SAM/ITAM risks should be consistent with business, corporate and IT risk management processes. The three main steps are:

■ **Risk identification** The creation of a register of identified risks from those events that could have a negative impact on the achievement of objectives.
■ **Risk assessment and evaluation** The analysis and understanding of the risks and the subsequent evaluation of each risk, its probability, threat

and impact so that each risk within the register can be assigned a relative priority.

■ **Risk treatment** Determining the appropriate action to manage the risk. This could be by:

● mitigating the risk: by changing the likelihood of it occurring; changing its consequences; or by sharing it with another party

● removing the source of the risk

● avoiding the risk by removing the activity that gives rise to it

● taking or increasing the risk to exploit an opportunity

● accepting the risk by informed decision.

Within the risk management area there should be:

■ a defined owner for each risk, responsible for managing the risk

■ criteria for the assessment of risk

■ criteria for the acceptance of a risk

■ criteria for the criticality of assets

■ regular review, analysis and assessment of risks and risk register(s)

■ regular prioritization and re-prioritization of risk(s) and their treatment(s) (because risks are dynamic and will change with time and events, such as result from technology changes). Residual risks should also be continually reviewed and managed.

An annual refresh of the organization's risk register should inform it of potential risks, and the SAM/ITAM programme should be identified as a key mitigator of those risks where appropriate. Likewise, a SAM/ITAM manager should be communicating new risks to the business as they are recognized.

10.4 LIFECYCLE MANAGEMENT PROCESSES FOR IT ASSETS

10.4.1 Overview

The lifecycle management processes are used to manage assets throughout their lifecycles and are shown in Figure 10.3.

The stages in the lifecycle of an asset will depend on the type of asset, so not every asset will go

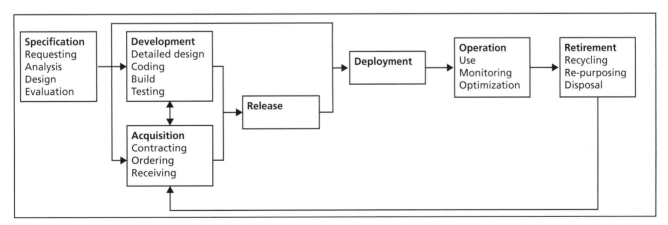

Figure 10.3 Lifecycle management processes for IT assets

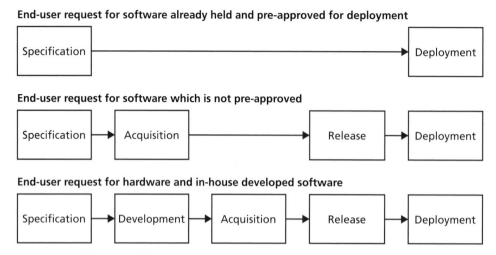

Figure 10.4 Some typical IT asset lifecycle variations

through the same stages. Some example asset lifecycles are shown in Figure 10.4; the definitions may vary between organizations.

The lifecycle processes are described in the following sub-sections. Additional information on some of these process areas can also be found in *ITIL Service Transition* and *ITIL Service Operation* (2011).

10.4.2 Specification process

10.4.2.1 Overview

Purpose

To accurately identify, analyse, design, evaluate, agree and document the asset requirements for any new or changed IT service requirement.

The specification process for SAM/ITAM could also be called requirements definition. More information on the definition and evaluation of requirements can be found in section 5.1 (requirements engineering) of *ITIL Service Design*.

This section discusses the specification process in terms of its component sub-processes or activities, namely:

- requesting
- analysis
- high-level design
- evaluation.

Each organization determines the number of approval stages required for the overall process (e.g. a requisition might require approval from end-user management before being submitted to IT), but the final specification must always be approved.

There must be appropriate documentation, both of the final specification and of its approval. Again, each organization should determine the level of documentation required within the process.

The final deliverable of the specification process should include: functional, non-functional and usability requirements; the business justification; the selected way of meeting the requirements; and the source of funding.

10.4.2.2 Requesting

New requirements for assets are typically triggered in one of three ways:

- a service request
- a change request
- a new business initiative.

If SAM/ITAM activities are being integrated with ITSM processes there will already be existing processes for handling these items. Each should be assessed for their impact on SAM/ITAM processes and disciplines.

Service requests

Request fulfilment is the process of handling requests for IT products and services from users. However, establishing SAM/ITAM best practice could provide increased benefit by considering:

- Can requests only be raised from a preferred set of products/services?
- Are standard requests pre-approved?
- Do requests get vetted against the available licence pool prior to being passed to an acquisition process?
- Do requests require managerial approval?
- Do requests require IT approval?

Decisions on the first three items in this bullet list will reduce the bureaucracy and increase the efficiency of fulfilling requests for additional assets. Use of the bullet list should also cut down on those requests that are made because 'a colleague has a software title, therefore I need it'. IT approval could prevent titles that have already been retired/deleted from reappearing on the IT estate; and assessing whether the organization has already bought a software title could reduce IT spend through utilizing existing licences from the available pool.

While these steps may seem overly bureaucratic (and indeed for a manual/paper driven process that could well be the case), increasingly, SAM/ITAM tools can interact with other systems, such as workflow management engines. This integration can drive greater automation, such as the approval/denial required for asset requests.

Change requests

It is also likely that there is an existing change management process. Every release/deployment of new or changed assets into the operational environment should be initiated by a change request. This includes the upgrade, downgrade or move of software or hardware assets. From a SAM/ITAM perspective, such changes should be validated from a licensing point of view prior to any changes taking place, with verification that any updates are made to the right quantity and specific devices that require the change.

Moves of software should not be disregarded, including in the data centre. The near-dizzying speed with which virtual devices can be generated and then have software installed is frightening. This means that due diligence around whether that software will be supported by the original licence could easily be skimped for the sake of delivering live services. Ignore this step at your peril!

Change requests should also be raised for asset retirement and disposal so that appropriate updates can be made to asset management records (see section 10.4.8).

Business initiatives

Major new business initiatives (or change proposals), such as the development of new products, implementation of new or changed business processes or the creation of new business units, will almost certainly require the acquisition of new assets. These will require extensive assessment and analysis, and are normally the subject of a complete value business case and a dedicated project or programme. SAM/ITAM people and processes will need to interact closely with these initiatives to ensure that asset requirements are accurately assessed and approved. This will not only require the accurate capturing of information on assets but also the accurate analysis and agreeing of the management requirements for those assets, especially where new hardware or software is acquired.

10.4.2.3 Analysis

Analysis should determine possible ways to meet the requirements specified in the request and which of these should be investigated further.

If sufficient assets already exist within the organization, the first consideration is whether to satisfy the request from:

- spare software licences (pre-purchased and/or reclaimed/recycled), or
- hardware assets that can be re-purposed or recycled.

If there are sufficient licences and resources and no new assets are required, much of the acquisition process can be skipped for fulfilment of this request. The same applies if the request is fairly basic, relatively inexpensive and will not create unusual risks.

It is at this point that the requirements for new or changed software or configurations need to be identified. If there are none, then the development processes of the lifecycle may be skipped.

10.4.2.4 High-level design

After analysis, a high-level design of the solution should be produced. This stage has historically focused primarily on technical design, but it is increasingly recognized as being a critical stage for almost all the areas potentially impacted by IT solutions. Three concepts are particularly applicable at this stage:

- **Security by design** Security cannot be expected to be effective if it is 'bolted-on' to a solution later in the development process.
- **Privacy by design** Legislation in some jurisdictions now mandates the principle of privacy by design for systems handling personal data.
- **Licensing by design** Licensing must be considered at this stage. It is particularly relevant where client–server architectures are involved, because the licensing implications of technical decisions can be significant.

Alternative designs may be identified (e.g. other architectures which could be used), and alternative solutions to a particular design (e.g. different publishers for a specific architecture).

The final design should include a high-level summary of the costs of the solution and should identify the budgets that will be used to pay for it.

10.4.2.5 Evaluation

The evaluation stage consists of reviewing the high-level design for:

- the scale and appropriateness of the solution
- the level of the costs and whether they are within budget
- whether the proposed solution complies with existing policies (e.g. concerning standard architectures and preferred suppliers).

Additional authorization might be needed to approve the design for the use of non-preferred assets and suppliers or where the budget is insufficient.

Once the appropriate authorizations have been obtained then the next stage (development and/or acquisition) can be initiated, or in some cases deployment may take place immediately.

10.4.3 Acquisition process

Purpose
To ensure that IT assets are properly acquired, with business justification and in a cost-effective manner.

The acquisition process for SAM/ITAM is covered in principle by some of the ITIL processes, in particular aspects of supplier management in *ITIL Service Design* and of request fulfilment in *ITIL Service Operation*. However, there are so many special requirements related to software and licensing, including ensuring the receipt of authentic products and valid proof of licence, that the subject is addressed separately in this guide.

This section discusses the acquisition process in terms of its component sub-processes or activities, namely:

■ contracting
■ ordering
■ receiving.

Ordering and receiving are part of an overall process flow as shown in Figure 10.5.

This stage of the IT asset lifecycle is primarily for acquiring externally sourced assets and is entered once the specification process has been completed and the most appropriate solution selected and authorized. It may also be necessary to complete some of the activities within this stage for in-house developed software if hardware assets or additional software assets are required (e.g. development software or additional software and/or licences for the live environment).

Acquisition can also be used to obtain internally sourced assets. If hardware assets already exist within the organization, acquisition will consist of ensuring they can be taken from the appropriate

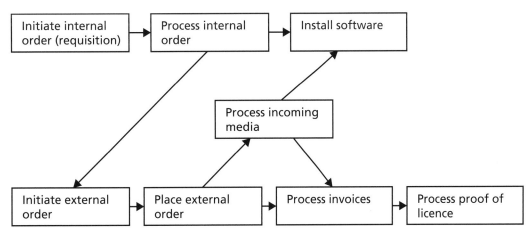

Figure 10.5 The SAM/ITAM acquisition process

secure storage areas and raising the necessary request(s) for their extraction. Likewise, if master copies of software already exist within the organization, they can be used subject to normal release and deployment controls. The situation is more complex with respect to licences, since many licence agreements allow for the purchase of licences after they are used, typically monthly or yearly.

If additional IT assets need to be acquired from (or contracts placed with) external organizations, then the following process stages will be required.

10.4.3.1 Contracting

This stage will only be required if no suitable contract already exists.

If contracting is required, this stage should include the selection of the most cost-effective partners and suppliers.

Supplier management and legal involvement is needed to ensure that the right negotiations and contracts are put in place with any new suppliers. Any new contracts should include standard terms and conditions wherever possible.

10.4.3.2 Ordering

Conceptually, there is a need for separate activities relating to initiating an external order and actually placing it. This is because initiation creates the commitment to order, but the actual placement of the order may depend on the organization's own policies and procedures (e.g. orders may only be placed daily or weekly), or on contractual terms and conditions (e.g. some agreements require reporting only monthly or yearly, in what is called a 'true-up'). While true-up order requirements can be determined as one-off exercises at the time the order needs to be placed, it is best practice to maintain an authoritative count of what will need to be reported so as to avoid unexpectedly high expenditure at true-up time, and as a check on the integrity of the ordering and inventory processes.

A consistent finding in many organizations is that there is poor coordination of purchasing arrangements, with the result that purchases are often made that do not take advantage of the best available alternatives. For example, a business unit may purchase a product locally at retail prices rather than through a centralized and more cost-effective contract. The process for initiating the external order should ensure that the most appropriate source is chosen for fulfilling the order.

10.4.3.3 Receiving

Receiving must ensure the receipt both of goods (hardware and media for software) and of proof of licence where relevant. (Media may be physical or electronic.) Receiving must also make reasonable efforts to ensure the authenticity of products received (i.e. that they are not counterfeit, pirated or tainted). Tainted products can include grey market hardware with compromised hardware or firmware, which can present not only major security risks but risks such as poor product quality and lack of manufacturer support.

Software presents the greatest challenges for receiving, in particular when it is purchased via resellers rather than directly from the publisher. This includes the requirement for ensuring receipt of the proof of licence. One complication is the fact that many volume-licensing situations involve a tripartite relationship, with the order going to a reseller, but the licence confirmation coming back from the software publisher. It is possible to insist on receiving the licence confirmation before payment, but this

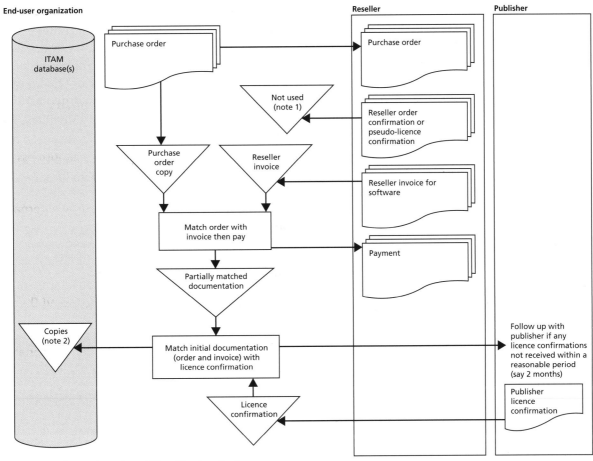

Note 1: Not used – not relevant for matching with order or invoice
Note 2: Copy all proof of licence documents including licence confirmation

Figure 10.6 Checking receipt of publisher proof of licence

will often be problematical because of the impact it will have on reseller cash flow. As a result, an alternative procedure can be used (Figure 10.6).

Publisher licence confirmations are typically now available online, and therefore they should be available fairly soon after orders are submitted to resellers. However, there may be a delay if the reseller batches orders and does not submit them to the publisher when received from the end-user.

Checking for the authenticity of products received, and in particular for software, can also present challenges. There is a significant risk of organizations purchasing counterfeit software through non-volume-licensing channels. In part, this is because of (a) the attractiveness of this market to counterfeiters, and (b) the limited attention often paid to product authenticity by end-user organizations, and sometimes even by resellers and distributors. The purchasing organization should make reasonable checks for software authenticity, especially when risk factors for counterfeiting are elevated.

> **Warning**
>
> The biggest 'red flag' for counterfeit software is low price.
>
> If one reseller charges significantly less than another reseller for the same quantity of the same product, beware of counterfeits. Explanations of 'grey imports' or 'clearance stock' are likely to be deceptions.
>
> Ensure that a breakdown of hardware and software costs is obtained for any package deals offered.

The licence confirmation may be physical or electronic, and there can be issues of authenticity about physical licence confirmations as well, if they are not received directly from the software publisher. There have been cases of counterfeit physical volume-licensing confirmations.

10.4.4 Development process

Purpose

To ensure that all IT assets are developed to conform to all organizational policies and all legal and regulatory requirements.

The development process for SAM/ITAM is not covered by ITIL but is part of the IT asset lifecycle, so an overview of it needs to be included here. This section highlights some of the SAM/ITAM issues to be considered as part of the process. Variants of the 'pure' development process, such as DevOps, will need to be taken into account when designing the ITAMS for any particular organization.

Development includes more than coding. It also includes configuration activities for commercial off-the-shelf (COTS) software. For example, default accounts may need to be deleted or have their passwords changed. The majority of COTS software just requires configuring to fit the organization's needs. These actions are all part of the build stage of the lifecycle.

The development process can be viewed in terms of its component sub-processes or activities, namely:

- detailed design
- coding
- build and configuration
- testing.

A few issues that are relevant to development, and particularly important for SAM/ITAM and licence compliance in particular, are:

- the use of open-source code. This can create not only security issues (because of the challenges of ensuring that all security updates are incorporated) but also ones of licensing. Many different open-source licences exist, some of which may be unacceptable to many organizations (e.g. they may require the public release of all source code developed on the basis of that original code).
- the control of licensing for machines used in development. In general, software used to manage and perform actual development work is performing a 'production' role relative to the purpose of such software (i.e. to do development) and therefore needs to be licensed for production use. However, the software (such as databases) which is being used to support the software being developed will generally be licensed differently, for development purposes only.

- the licensing requirements for software post-release. Once software has been developed and tested and is ready for release into live production, its licensing requirements will often change dramatically, from the generally low-cost development licensing, into full production licensing. A common problem is that development and test configurations start being used for production purposes without correct licensing arrangements being in place.

10.4.5 Release process

Purpose

To ensure all releases of IT assets are properly authorized for deployment, including having been approved, and tested as necessary.

The release process for SAM/ITAM is the first half of the release and deployment management process for ITSM, as described in *ITIL Service Transition*. Reference should be made there for detailed guidance.

The release and deployment processes are identified separately in ITAM because they are typically performed separately for most mass-deployment software. In particular, ensuring that a product is ready for deployment into the live environment (i.e. is released) is done only once for each product/update/configuration, but deployment happens numerous times based on potentially varied deployment mechanisms.

The release process is initiated once everything prior to final approval for deployment has been completed. If software had to be developed or configured, that should already have been successfully tested. If something has been purchased which does not require configuration (e.g. certain hardware assets), then it may come directly to the release process.

At this stage of the lifecycle many organizations undertake further testing in additional environments (such as pre-production and staging). Potentially, this is where live integration and performance testing are performed, and user acceptance testing activities are also completed. This ensures that all the components within the release work together effectively. It may also be necessary to check that this release works effectively with other systems and services, so additional integration testing may be needed to be undertaken with those.

The release process should ensure that:

- the release consists of only those components that are authorized for inclusion in the release package
- all release components are authentic and supported
- all required licences are held (e.g. database licences are in place)
- all master copies of software and licences are stored in the DML
- all assets can be effectively managed in the live environment
- all the operation, management and support documentation for the release is complete and effective
- all relevant asset information within the CMS is accurate and up to date
- all spare assets are stored within secure storage facilities.

If these testing and checking activities are successful then approval will be given for the release to be deployed to the authorized live environments; if unsuccessful, it may be necessary to refer the release back for further development or acquisition activities.

10.4.6 Deployment process

Purpose

To ensure that all deployments have first been properly released (i.e. authorized for deployment), and are deployed only as specifically authorized.

The deployment process for SAM/ITAM is the second half of the release and deployment management process for ITSM as described in *ITIL Service Transition*. Reference should be made there for detailed guidance.

As mentioned in section 10.4.5, the release and deployment processes are identified separately in ITAM because they are typically performed separately for most mass-deployment software.

Deployment processes should ensure that:

■ the deployment is authorized (either specifically or via general policies)
■ all proposed destination environments are covered by the necessary contracts and licences
■ all proposed destination environments are suitable and have sufficient space and resources to support the release
■ the integrity of the release, and all assets contained within the release, are protected throughout the deployment activities.

If business initiatives require the deployment (i.e. installation) of COTS software in live environments, it should be closely monitored to ensure that any grace period for reporting that might be granted before it is deemed to be live (and therefore licensable) is not exceeded.

Software licence agreements often allow installation and use of software before licences are purchased periodically (e.g. monthly or yearly). However, an organization must still be able to prove it has a valid licence for each piece of software installed. Whether this is tackled retrospectively (after the installation) or proactively (before the installation) is a judgement call for each organization, the most important point being that it does take place.

10.4.7 Operation process

Purpose

To ensure that all IT assets within the operational environment conform and continue to conform to all SAM/ITAM, legal and regulatory requirements; that all exceptions are referred to the appropriate areas for action; and that the use of IT assets is optimized as practicable.

The operation process for SAM/ITAM is not covered by ITIL, although there is a description of the IT operations management function in *ITIL Service Operation*. Reference should be made there for guidance.

Operation is clearly part of IT infrastructure management and is one of the main differentiators between server-side and client-side infrastructure management. The former is generally associated with data centre management, whereas the latter is generally associated with SAM/ITAM, notwithstanding that the discipline should include both sides. On the server side, there is generally a direct operation role on the part of operations staff. On the client side, end-users perform much of this role.

This stage of the SAM/ITAM lifecycle includes all the daily routine tasks, processes and activities necessary for the successful monitoring and managing of the operation of all live environments. It should also be responsible for ensuring that all other environments (e.g. development, testing and staging) are also correctly monitored, managed and maintained for compliance. All operational services, IT infrastructure and software should, wherever possible, be automatically monitored and controlled, with all exceptions triggering alerts/alarms.

The operation process typically iinvolves:

- monitoring all operational services and systems for alerts, warnings, errors, failures and exceptions, ensuring that they are referred to the appropriate individuals and areas for remedial action
- control of secure storage areas and access to them, ensuring that they contain the appropriate levels of space and resources
- maintenance and housekeeping of secure storage areas and the CMS, including monitoring their usage and status for issues and actions, taking regular back-ups and maintaining access controls
- reporting, both scheduled and ad hoc, on physical and electronic secure storage facilities and related information on their usage
- executing recovery procedures when required.

Additionally, the operation function should address the issue of optimization. All organizations should attempt to optimize the use of assets wherever it is practical to do so. One of the major ways of achieving this is through the recycling, re-purposing and reuse of assets.

Other activities that can be used to optimize the resources and assets used by SAM/ITAM processes are:

- assessing, reviewing, monitoring and reporting on all operational activities and processes to ensure that they are continually improved
- regularly monitoring and reviewing the status of relevant physical and electronic secure storage facilities for risks, issues and threats and addressing them, where necessary

- reviewing all SAM/ITAM operational tools, processes, activities and tasks on a regular basis, and recommending and instigating appropriate improvements.

10.4.8 Retirement process

Purpose

To ensure that all IT assets retired from use (including both hardware and software) are processed in compliance with organizational policies and legal/regulatory requirements; which may include recycling, re-purposing or disposal.

The retirement process for SAM/ITAM does not have an equivalent in ITIL. Retirement of services is frequently mentioned in ITIL as a type of change which requires change management, but the concepts of recycling, re-purposing and disposal of assets are only covered briefly.

Retirement of software is an aspect of SAM/ITAM that is perhaps not as well practised as it should be. Just because software is no longer installed, does not mean it should be ignored. Major software publishers have been known to reserve the right to audit end-user organizations up to 2 years after the last installation has been removed, so vigilance around ensuring such retired titles do not creep back into use is a worthwhile exercise.

This is where there is real value in creating and maintaining an up-to-date SSC and an SHC. Those titles which are deemed retired (not installed, but which could be recalled at a later stage) should be appropriately flagged so that end-users are not allowed to request them as new installations. Proof of licence for such titles should be ear-marked for archiving at an appropriate cut-off date before their use is finally deemed to have been abandoned.

One of the most cost-effective and underrated means of making better use of IT budgets is the process of software recycling and re-purposing. If a software installation has not been used after a given period of time, which is typically 90 days for production installations and 30 days for testing/development installations (licensing terms and conditions typically dictate the relevant minimum periods) then a SAM/ITAM imperative should be to remove it. This not only re-stocks the available licence pool from purchases already made, it also prevents test and development installations being counted as live if the trial period of installation is exceeded.

Example

A FTSE 100 company in the UK embarked upon a SAM/ITAM implementation and, as part of the process, established harvesting, recycling and re-purposing procedures. These procedures included the monitoring of savings made from the removal of unused licences and their subsequent reuse. The savings made from these software harvesting activities alone were in excess of £500,000. From that point on it was much easier to get approval and support from the CIO and senior management for additional SAM/ITAM activities.

Certain titles might be considered exempt from the standard 90-day removal rule (e.g. installations for executives, or software only used at specific points in the year), so remain flexible when designing and implementing this process.

Important

Do not wait for a compliance report to be produced before you start thinking about removing software. Your primary criteria for its removal should be one of non-use, not compliance.

Disposing of software goes hand in hand with the business decision of retirement, but so does hardware disposal. Change requests should be raised for all asset removal, retirement and disposal so that appropriate updates can be made to the asset management records. If devices have reached the end of their useful life within the organization, there will probably be legal or regulatory obligations to ensure that all information is comprehensively deleted from them before they are physically destroyed or recycled.

One aspect of disposal that often gets overlooked within SAM/ITAM is the checking of asset management systems to ensure that the relevant records are archived or purged. If this is overlooked, the ITAMS will merely report that the device is missing; it cannot reasonably be expected to know that such devices have been removed and possibly destroyed. Removing these devices from ITAMS should then free up the software licences that were attributed to them, thereby re-stocking the available licence pool.

Certificates are required for IT asset disposal (ITAD) in some countries, and ITAD organizations around the globe who claim professionalism in this area should provide them. When these certificates are received by an organization, they should be used as a means of verifying that devices have been removed from the asset estate. The change request should only be signed off and closed once the disposal certificate has been received for each retired asset.

It may be worth checking to ensure that the disposed devices have not unwittingly become available on an auction website to cause the organization public embarrassment or (worse still) a personal data/information security breach that could result in substantial fines or court cases.

10.5 THE 1-2-3 OF SAM/ITAM BUSINESS AS USUAL

A way of monitoring the effectiveness of SAM/ITAM processes is by monitoring the relationships between software recorded as deployed, software discovered as actually deployed, and licences held. Figure 10.7 offers guidance on how to keep wastage to a minimum during business as usual (BaU).

The 1-2-3 of SAM/ITAM BaU involves addressing the following:

■ Unlicensed software (Area 1 in Figure 10.7). Identify software that is installed (and in the approved software catalogue) but has no proof of licence to account for it. Aside from finding or obtaining proof of licence to mitigate those 'rogue' installations, root-cause analysis may also be required to understand how the software was installed onto the IT estate in the first place (if it did not come through established change management procedures).

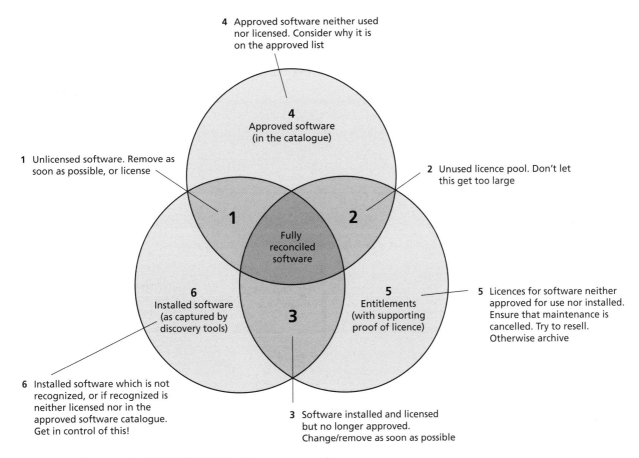

Figure 10.7 The 1-2-3 of SAM/ITAM business as usual

- Software that is licensed (and in the approved software catalogue) but not installed (Area 2 in Figure 10.7). This is the licence pool, which should not get too large. Most organizations have some degree of reserve software; how much is tolerated is for each organization to decide. You must be prepared to justify its size to senior management.
- Software that is installed (and has proof of licence) but does not appear in the approved software catalogue (Area 3 in Figure 10.7). This is probably old software which has been missed in migrations or upgrades. It may present security risks and also increased costs for support.

Beyond the top three, a further three can be identified:

- Software that is in the approved software catalogue but is neither used nor licensed (Area 4 in Figure 10.7). This should be reviewed; the software probably needs to be deleted from the catalogue.
- Licences held for software which is neither approved for use nor installed (Area 5 in Figure 10.7). This is probably for obsolete software. Ensure that maintenance is cancelled. It should be resold or archived.
- Installed software which is neither licensed nor in the approved software catalogue (Area 6 in Figure 10.7). Some of this software may simply be unrecognized by the SAM/ITAM discovery tool. If so, it could be malware and represent a major security threat. Alternatively, it may be recognized, but is neither licensed nor in the approved software catalogue. This may create many types of risk, but of software underlicensing risk in particular. Get it under control!

Products: tools and technology

11

11 Products: tools and technology

The purpose of this chapter is to give an overview of the technology of ITAM tools and databases. It is not intended as a guide for defining database contents, which is covered in Appendix E, but it does give hints on establishing an overall strategy for an organization's use of ITAM technology.

ITAM technology has advanced considerably in recent years, a process that will certainly continue in the future. There have been many drivers behind its development, including:

- the recognition that there is much more to be managed, and it is generally more complex than what went before it (cloud and BYOD being two major examples)
- the emergence of new focus areas for technology, such as identity and access management
- the development of more specialist tools to provide niche functionality, such as measuring usage for specific publishers or technologies
- the creation of new ISO standards, which are starting to have a major impact, especially for quality of information, improved interoperability between tools, and the opportunity for increased automation in security and licence management (see Appendix D).

Complexity has always been an issue in ITAM. As soon as ITAM tools start to cope with some areas of complexity, new ones arise, so the vertical learning curve and vertical coping curve will almost certainly continue. Tools cannot eliminate these complexities, only help to make them easier to understand and manage. Spreadsheet tools by themselves, in particular, should be seen as red flags indicating overly simplistic approaches to ITAM. Such tools generally cannot be considered adequate in any but the simplest and smallest of environments (however, there is still a place for simple technology; see section 11.5).

Key message

ITAM technology is similar to accounting technology. First, in theory both are simple; in reality they are not. Secondly, both are essential parts of the 'solution', but nonetheless only small parts. It is not possible to run a successful organization simply by buying and installing a good accounting system; you need well-developed operational and management practices, including regular audits, to make it all work well. The same is true for ITAM systems. You cannot manage IT assets without good ITAM tools, but those tools contribute just a fraction of what must be done, on a continuing basis, to have a well-functioning ITAMS. Ask your CFO and chief executive officer (CEO) how much effort it takes them personally, and the organization as well, to achieve the data integrity required, and the intended results, from their accounting system. Both types of system are essentially for record-keeping, but their purposes are to facilitate good management, not just the number-crunching of untrustworthy data.

11.1 ITAM TECHNOLOGY STRATEGY

11.1.1 Overview

An organization's use of ITAM technology, and in particular its selection of ITAM tools and databases, does not happen in a vacuum. It is essential to have an overall strategy concerning what is needed, and this strategy needs to be driven by business requirements and the need to drive business value. It is recommended that organizations consider the following in determining an ITAM technology strategy.

11.1.2 Scope and priorities

Do not attempt too much. The scope of an ITAM project needs to be clearly defined, and it is far better to start small, obtain good results, and then expand later. The highest priority or priorities should determine the initial scope (subject to something even smaller done first as a pilot or trial). If the priority is licence compliance, the likely choice for initial scope is going to be the publisher which presents the greatest audit exposure. If, however, that publisher is technically complex, it might be better to start with one with less technical and licensing complexity.

It is still worthwhile considering the longer-range scope, to have reasonable confidence that the tools chosen will suffice, but the immediate implementation should focus on the highest priorities rather than on everything at once.

Note that if the priority is security and security automation, a different set of tools may be more suitable based on those packages cited in association with the CSCs (see Chapter 14). In particular, there is a limited set of security-focused tools which have functionality generally recognized as relevant for licence compliance.

The need for recording authorizations is increasingly being recognized both for security and for licence management. Including such requirements in any scope definition is probably justifiable (see also section 14.2).

11.1.3 Identification of required data and infrastructure complexities

Once priorities are clarified and the scope defined, the data needed to support that scope should be identified. This is particularly relevant if licence compliance is a priority and the publisher covered uses metrics requiring data which is not collected by some ITAM packages.

Likewise, the types of infrastructure to be supported should be identified. This should address issues like virtualization, cloud services, mobile devices, clustering, big data requirements, international and global delivery requirements, and the potential diversity of publishers and platforms.

Potentially, a data model could be constructed to specify the required data. Appendix E can be used to facilitate this work. As stated above, do not attempt too much (including requirements which are just 'nice-to-have').

11.1.4 Assessment of existing tools and capabilities

Do not assume that you will need to purchase a new tool. It is likely that your organization has already purchased multiple tools which will provide some or much of the functionality you require. They may already be in use, but not for your purposes. They may have been purchased but never implemented. They may have been implemented, but fallen out of use. If existing tools can meet your requirements (except in one or two specialist areas, such as measuring usage for a particular publisher), consider obtaining a 'point' solution just for this requirement. Another alternative is to consider outsourced ITAM services for the required capabilities.

Wherever possible any ITAM tools should be part of an overall management tool architecture. Leading organizations have a management tool architecture to ensure that:

- there is little overlap or duplication of functionality between tools
- there is agreement on which tools provide the storage and management information within each area
- the tools together provide support for a complete and integrated management system for all areas.

11.1.5 Requirements for continuing operations and maintenance

Be sure to consider requirements for continuing operations and maintenance. It is not enough simply to install a tool. Indeed, tools previously installed may have fallen out of use because not enough resources were provided to keep them operational.

11.2 ITAM DATABASES

This chapter discusses the various databases and management systems which are relevant within ITAM and ITSM (and ITIL in particular). It should be noted that terminology may be used in contradictory ways by people in different specialisms. This guide states clearly that the ITAM repositories are part of the overall CMDBs within the CMS. Nonetheless, some people working in the area of ITSM sometimes express the view that the information about client-side assets (e.g. PCs and related software) is excluded from, and therefore held outside, the CMDBs. This

guide takes the more inclusive view of the organization's data, while recognizing that the CMDBs are federated and not a single database.

Figure 11.1 provides an overview of the databases and libraries used by ITSM, ITAM and also information security management, to help clarify by example what is typically held in each, and how they relate to each other. All stages of the lifecycles are interdependent. The SKMS provides the central backbone repository for the sharing of information between all processes and across all lifecycle stages.

It is unlikely that a single unitary ITAM database will ever exist; however, the ITAM database(s) will probably be federated, with each individual database equivalent to a free-standing CMDB, all of which are part of the ITAM CMS (which itself is effectively part of the ITIL CMS). This follows both from practical observations and from a recognition that the 'one source of all truth' approach is impractical either to design or to implement. It would be one of the worst examples of a 'big-bang' approach to ITAM system design, an approach which this guide strongly discourages.

In practice this means that organizations should expect to have multiple tools, potentially with their own databases. Tools and databases should be chosen to maximize interoperability and consolidation of information. To the extent that the suite of tools offered by a provider grows by adding multiple tool functionalities, it offers an opportunity for improved interoperability and consolidation of information from its different components. However, there is still a major issue relating to interoperability between tools from different providers. This is particularly evident in those situations where an organization with multiple units, using many different tools from multiple providers, needs to consolidate that information for overall reporting purposes, such as

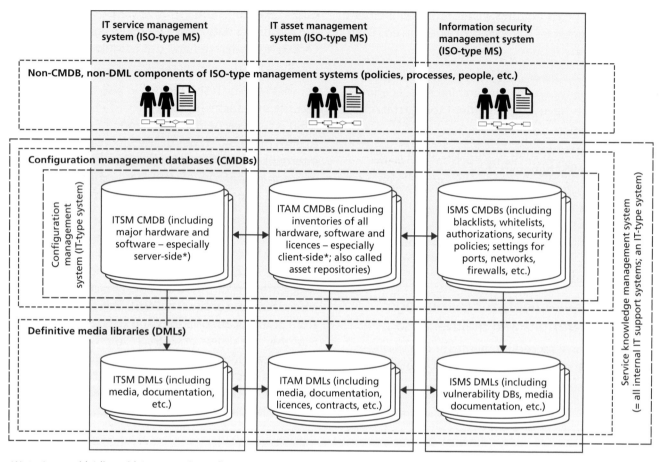

*Note: 'server-side/client-side' contents just reflect common usage, and are not mandated by the concepts

Figure 11.1 Databases and libraries used by ITSM, ITAM and information security management

for a publisher licensing audit. The fairly new ISO standards for software identification and entitlements will increasingly drive such interoperability, and the normalization of data values. This should also reduce tool provider lock-in, so that tools can be assessed based on their functionality rather than on problems related to migration (see Appendix D).

Note that, typically, service management tools will make use of the ITAM databases as the foundation of the ITIL CMS (see section 11.3).

Appendix E provides some suggestions about what information could be included in ITAM databases.

11.3 CENTRALIZATION OR DECENTRALIZATION OF SAM/ITAM DATABASES

Each organization must decide how to implement its SAM/ITAM database, both logically and physically. The decision has major time and cost implications.

In theory, the centralized functions described above would best be supported by a centralized SAM/ITAM database. However, this may not be practical for a number of reasons:

- The parent company is a holding company that buys and sells subsidiaries frequently.
- Different subsidiaries or business units operate largely autonomously, and a centralized SAM/ITAM database would require an unacceptable level of operational centralization.
- The diverse and frequently changing ways of measuring usage against licence entitlements often require 'point solutions' for those specific measurement requirements.

The following approach is therefore recommended:

- The SAM/ITAM database should be implemented as an integrated, centralized database to the extent practical. In principle, this should be at the level that corresponds to operational IT responsibility, so there would be a consolidated SAM/ITAM database for each area of autonomous IT responsibility. Responsibility for licence compliance should also be clearly defined at this level. Furthermore, physical proof of licence should be controlled at this level.
- SAM/ITAM should be implemented in achievable modules or projects. For global organizations, realizing a truly centralized position can take years.

- Information from the separate federated SAM/ITAM databases must be provided to central functions on a regular and consistent basis to allow them to perform properly.
- Each SAM/ITAM database may be a single physically integrated repository or a collection of free-standing but linked databases (a 'shared data environment') utilizing the capabilities of different systems and tools. Full integration is desirable but not easily achievable given the current state of the market for SAM/ITAM and related tools.

11.4 ITAM TOOLS

11.4.1 Overview

Figure 11.2 gives an overview of the ITAM technology architecture. It includes the major types of tool available, each of which is separately discussed in this chapter. Many other tools are available to support and manage the IT infrastructure, for example to cover ITIL areas such as incident and problem management. A discussion of those tools is beyond the scope of this guide, but their generic class is shown in Figure 11.2 by the box 'service management tools'. As stated previously, all these tools should be part of an overall management tool architecture to ensure end-to-end management functionality is provided across the complete IT infrastructure, with agreed areas of responsibility for provision of 'master data' in each area.

11.4.2 Asset inventory tools

Asset inventory tools are the essential foundation of all SAM/ITAM activity. At the simpler end of the spectrum, a spreadsheet may constitute such a tool in a very small organization. However, a more extensive solution is almost always required.

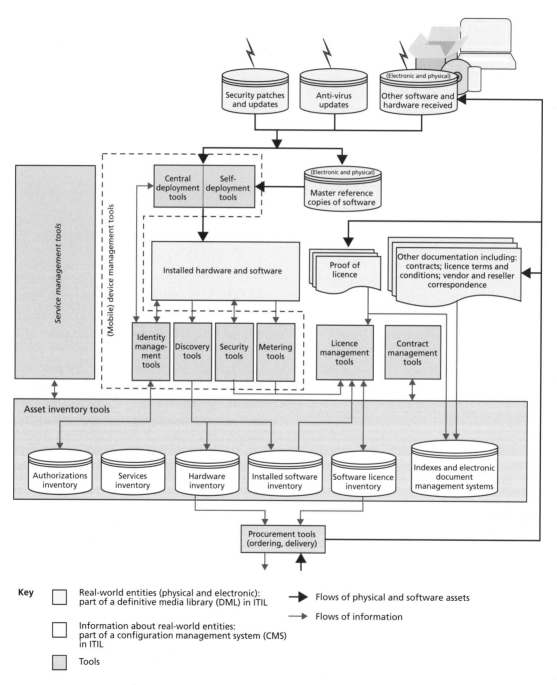

Figure 11.2 ITAM technology architecture

Available software tools vary considerably in their functionality. At the top end, they are typically integrated with other functionality. Three broad categories of asset inventory functionality can be identified:

- **Inventories of hardware and installed software** These are the most common types of tool and are often integrated with, or designed to work with, discovery tools.
- **Inventories of software licences** Available functionality for managing software licences is comparatively limited. Tools for inventories of hardware and installed software may include some licence inventory functionality. There are also more specialist licences management applications available. Basic functionality includes the linking of different types of licence purchased to determine the current effective licences available for use, and where the use of the licence is assigned. Other functionality can support procurement functions including the reallocation of licences between different operational units. Note that the ISO standard ISO/IEC 19770-3 (Entitlement schema) facilitates normalized data values and interoperability between tools, plus support for many of the specific requirements of licence management, such as allocations to different units (see Appendix D).
- **Document management systems** Physical documentation such as contracts and correspondence also needs to be managed and kept secure, as well as being made accessible. Electronic document management systems are best suited to doing this, allowing easy linking or cross-referencing to other database systems. Copies of physical proof of licence would typically also be held in the document management system, with the originals stored in a separate, secure location.

11.4.3 Discovery tools

Most discovery tools are designed to find hardware and installed software and collect relevant details about them. (There is also potential for a class of cloud service discovery tools; see section 4.5.) Discovery tools are used during an initial implementation, and also periodically during ongoing operations as part of data verification.

A large number of tools in the market address this area. Some of the major issues involved are:

- **Hardware (physical and virtual) and platforms** Different types of tool may be required to discover different physical and virtualized hardware and platforms. These include not only traditional client and server platforms, but also devices such as switches and routers.
- **Software by hardware/platform** Discovery tools need to be able to discover software on a range of platforms. Often an organization will have to use several different discovery tools because of the platform limitations of individual tools.
- **Networked versus non-networked use** Discovery tools are most efficient in a networked environment. However, there may be many machines that are seldom or never connected to a network, and methods must be found for getting information about these.
- **Agent-based versus agentless** Agent-based discovery tools have software (the agent) installed on each device to facilitate discovery on that device. Agentless tools work by scanning the entire network, and because there is no locally installed agent, there is a need for admin-level credentials to query each device. Current best practice is to use a combination of the two approaches.

■ **Method and reliability of software identification**
There are several methods of software identification, and tools may provide for a combination of them. In general, all approaches work well for major commercial applications developed and installed in accordance with industry standards. They are less helpful for in-house applications and much of the popular software that is commonly distributed via the internet, such as file-swapping and instant messaging programs, which an organization may wish to identify and remove. These methods include:

● **Signatures** Some discovery tools utilize 'signature' information about the names, sizes etc. of key files for particular applications. These tools depend on the signature information (contained within software recognition libraries) being updated to allow new software to be identified.

● **Registry entries** Much software now places entries in the system registry that can be read by discovery tools. Major commercial packages and installation routines do this. However, some other software does not comply.

● **Software identification tags** Well-designed commercial software that meets industry standards will now include small files ('tags') containing authoritative identification information that can be read by discovery software, without the need for signature files (see Appendix D). Programs that do not follow these standards will not be as easy to identify authoritatively.

■ **Ability to summarize complex data meaningfully** There can be huge complexity in the data gathered during discovery and how it needs to be interpreted, as the following examples make clear. An application may consist of hundreds or thousands of individual files, all covered by one licence. Alternatively, a single licence may be required for one file. Installations may be complete or partial. Applications may be uninstalled, but without removing all the relevant files. Updates and patches may be applied, potentially affecting large numbers of files. Discovery tools differ greatly in how user-friendly and accurate they are in identifying specific applications and the installation state of each one. Extensive manual effort may be required to turn the output of discovery tools into meaningful summary information.

The output from discovery tools is often used as the basis for licence compliance assessment. However, such an approach may give the wrong results if there is not a full understanding of how software is actually used and the relevant licensing terms and conditions. For example, an application may be installed on a server, where it would be discovered only once. However, it might be executed from the server by many people connected to it, each of whom might require a licence.

11.4.4 Metering tools

Metering tools, or usage tools as they are sometimes referred to, are intended to measure active usage of a software product. When used just for monitoring and reporting, they may be referred to as 'passive metering' tools. A number of tools are now capable of providing licence verification before the software products run, and these may be known as 'active metering' tools. Such tools may be stand-alone or form part of an integrated toolset. These tools require the same type of regular metric/signature updating as those for discovery. Metering will only produce meaningful information for those applications it has been set up to recognize.

Historically, metering tools are most closely associated with monitoring the usage of server-based applications. Some licences are sold with 'concurrent usage' rights, which means that there is a maximum number of people who can use the software at any one time. Metering tools can be effective at preventing usage which exceeds the number of licences owned, or alternatively by generating an exception condition to initiate corrective action.

Metering tools are increasingly being used to measure active usage on non-server devices, especially workstations. Some tools can even distinguish between active and minimized applications. Some demand management functionality can be viewed as an add-on capability for metering tools. With appropriate analysis, usage information can help identify software that is installed but not being actively used. Decisions may be taken to redeploy licences being unnecessarily tied up in this way, rather than purchase yet more licences when they are needed elsewhere.

A major consideration with metering tools is their performance overheads. Increasingly, there are also legal issues. Historically, in countries where there are strong employee rights or workers' councils, a metering tool may be considered as a way of controlling the individual. However, the major issue now is personal data protection legislation, which may cover metering data. The exact type of metering to be implemented may need to be assessed carefully, and depending on local legislation may need to be performed in consultation with legal counsel or the appropriate employee representative organizations.

11.4.5 Licence management tools

Licence management tools are potentially among the most important tools in a SAM/ITAM implementation. However, although there have been some significant recent developments in their functionality and capability, the state of the market is comparatively immature. In many organizations, licence management is largely manual and prone to error, if it is being done at all. Automation, to the extent that does exist, is often just for the simpler types of software licensing and usage information (e.g. from discovery or metering tools).

There are several types of functionality that may be considered necessary for a licence management tool. These include being able to:

- determine and track on a regular basis (without extensive manual work) the need for each type of licence, based on the appropriate usage criteria. For example, the need for licences may be based on the number of installed copies; the total number of users; the maximum number of concurrent users; or the number of connected printers
- assess the financial impact of licence compliance shortfalls
- demonstrate the effective licences held, which requires, for example, the linking of upgrade or maintenance licences with the underlying full original licences
- link licence requirements to effective licences (i.e. entitlements) held, and to report on licensing exceptions identified
- manage stocks of unused licences, and potentially negative stocks if licences only need to be ordered periodically, after the software has been installed

- facilitate the allocation of licences held to different operational units, and the transfer of licences e.g. for demergers.

Ideally, licence management should be at the level of individual licences, linking specific licences to where they are used. Doing this may require linking different volume licences for different quantities of licences in complex ways.

11.4.6 Contract management tools

Contract management information is likely to be integrated with licence management information, since many detailed licence management issues link in to overall contractual ones. It may also be integrated with financial purchasing software. The types of functionality needed in this area include:

- supplier and contracts database systems for the recording and management of contracts and suppliers, as detailed in section 4.7 on supplier management in *ITIL Service Design*
- warnings about automatic contract extensions or maintenance payments falling due, deadlines for internally initiated renewals etc.
- monitoring of total purchasing levels against agreements to ensure that relevant commitments or projections are being met, for pricing purposes
- monitoring of other contractual terms and conditions, such as the implementation and running of publisher licence management tools.

11.4.7 Deployment management tools

Deployment tool technology continues to advance. Deployment can be driven from IT and can also be initiated by users themselves, for standard pre-approved software using either 'push' or 'pull' technology. The issue for ITAM is to ensure that

deployments are properly authorized and that relevant deployment data is captured within the ITAM database. Increasingly, processes such as this link into identity management tools (see section 11.4.9).

11.4.8 Security tools

Several security issues, for which a number of tools are available, are particularly relevant to ITAM. There is considerable overlap between this area and that of security in general, and the two must be clearly coordinated for best results. Section 11.4.9 on identity management tools overlaps closely with this one.

- **Installation security tools** There are a number of approaches to controlling software installations and preventing unauthorized installations, some of which can be implemented at the operating system level. There are also some major packages that have extensive functionality for determining who can install and/or run which software. (Other ITAM functionalities may be also included, such as metering.)
- **Protection tools** Anti-virus software can be viewed as an ITAM concern, as can general protection measures meant to protect existing software assets from compromise. The main issue ITAM is to ensure that anti-virus and security patch update procedures are tightly integrated into the overall process for SAM/ITAM, so that updates are distributed quickly and reliably when needed.

11.4.9 Identity management tools

Identity management tools are also sometimes referred to as 'identity and access' management tools. They provide focused authorization functionality for other IT processes and tools. The increasing emphasis on such tools underscores the importance of the concept of authorization in IT operations, including for SAM/ITAM processes.

11.4.10 Procurement tools

Procurement is an important area for ITAM, and the number of procurement tools and solutions being developed that are targeted at ITAM benefits is expanding. Relevant capabilities include:

- maintaining relevant financial information needed for SAM/ITAM (e.g. purchase cost, maintenance cost and discount level)
- ability to check online for the availability of unused licences as part of the ordering process (e.g. checking within the immediate operating entity or even with affiliated organizations that may have spare transferable licences)
- automatic linking of ordered licences to relevant licensee (e.g. PCs or individuals) to avoid repeat work later.

11.4.11 Mobile device management tools

Tools for MDM are becoming well established in the marketplace. Their development has been driven by the need to perform, for mobile devices, the same types of function as for traditional IT assets. While the technologies they need to manage are slightly different, the required functions are largely equivalent. For example, an MDM tool may contain the functionality for identity management, deployment, discovery, metering and security. Security in such cases can include policy enforcement and wiping of the device if necessary.

MDM tools have also been adapted to handle laptops and desktops, so the more appropriate term might be, simply, 'device management'. In principle

there is nothing to stop this conceptual approach being used for the server side as well; it is just a question of packaging and naming.

11.5 ITAM LOW-TECH TOOLS

While hi-tech tools as described in Section 11.4 are essential for effective ITAM in all but the smallest organizations, we should not lose sight of the value which can be obtained from some low-tech tools as well. One of the simplest is the use of checklists, which have proven highly beneficial even in highly complex areas such as a surgery (LinkedIn, 2015).

11.6 PUBLISHER LICENCE MANAGEMENT TECHNOLOGY

The focus of this guide is on customer management of software assets, including licensing. However, there are also a number of technologies used directly by the publisher to help ensure proper licensing and use in accordance with terms and conditions. Ensuring that the software continues to run may have implications for the infrastructure. Most publishers have traditionally taken the view that licensing controls should not result in potential interruption to operations, but this has often created an exposure to unlicensed usage. Some of the approaches that aim to reduce this exposure but still minimize the impact on operational use are:

- **Licensing keys** These are the most common approach to publisher-managed usage (PMU), and generally the least effective at preventing unlicensed use. However, it may be possible to trace the source of keys on unauthorized copies, especially where each individual licence has a unique key. Unauthorized use may come to the attention of software publishers in many ways, such as technical support calls by users with problems, during internet connections to download updates and as a result of audits.

- **Publisher cloud storage of activation status** This approach is increasingly being used to minimize the risk of unauthorized use of software. It requires online activation, and the software can periodically validate that it is properly activated, again requiring an online check.

- **Hardware dongles** This is one of the simplest secure forms of licence management technology, with each program keyed to require a specific hardware dongle to be attached to the PC (or other equipment) for it to run. This is now quite rare.

- **Technical licence management** With this technology, electronic licence certificates are obtained centrally and distributed to individual PCs, users etc. as required. The product itself checks to see if the licence is available. Publishers may implement this type of technology to handle

different architectures and build in flexibility for unlicensed use (e.g. granting a grace period before enforcement or in cases where there is a licence certificate interruption). A licence server is usually required, either online for each execution or to provide a more permanent key that may be used when not connected.

- **Metering** With this technology, the licensed product itself does no checking, but rather an independent monitoring agent identifies its (requested) execution and can record usage and also prevent execution. There are many ways of bypassing this type of control, which may be partially addressed by protected logs that can be analysed (e.g. for completeness of time coverage).

- **Wrapper technology** This technology encapsulates an application that cannot otherwise be controlled by technical licence management, so that the wrapper software installed, together with the application, provides this functionality.

Partners **12**

12 Partners

'Partner' is used here in the sense of organizations involved in a business relationship or association with the user organization. Partners provide a large number of services which can help end-user organizations with SAM/ITAM, in particular by providing outsourcing and managed services which are becoming increasingly important. It is possible to find current information about many of these services by using a good internet search engine and entering key words or phrases such as 'software asset management', 'SAM', 'IT asset management', 'ITAM' or by going to the websites of major partners of any of the types listed below.

Potential types of partners include:

- software publishers
- hardware manufacturers
- resellers
- SAM/ITAM tool providers and implementers
- SAM/ITAM consultants
- SAM/ITAM outsourcers
- training organizations
- auditors
- IT research organizations
- professional and industry associations
- anti-piracy organizations.

Many partner organizations fulfil more than one of these roles.

The main types of deliverable available from partners are:

- SAM/ITAM guidance materials, including 'best-practice' guidelines
- SAM/ITAM consultancy
- outsourcing of SAM/ITAM processes and roles
- audits, reviews or assessments
- certification
- conferences and workshops
- licensing advice
- historical purchase records and effective licence calculations
- current purchase records
- directories and assessments of SAM/ITAM tools
- SAM/ITAM tools
- implementation assistance for SAM/ITAM tools.

Further guidance concerning partners is given in the appendices:

- Appendix F provides suggested criteria for selecting a SAM/ITAM partner
- Appendix G provides guidance on partner contracting issues.

Implementation

13

13 Implementation

Implementation (including improvement) projects and programmes are common in business and especially in IT. Implementation is a complex subject and cannot be discussed in isolation from the topics covered in the rest of this guide. In particular, implementation needs to be undertaken in the context of applying the nine guiding principles of *ITIL Practitioner Guidance* (see section 2.1.2) such as to keep it simple and to progress iteratively. Likewise, the CSFs discussed in section 7.5.1 need to be considered. These include having a project approach and having an incremental approach.

Each organization will typically have its own standard approaches for project and programme management, and it is not in the scope of this guide to cover that subject in detail. This chapter does, however, deal with some specific implementation issues, such as different project approaches and costs. In addition, two task lists are given, which may provide practical help to individuals tasked with starting an ITAM function or given the responsibility for creating a greatly expanded ITAM programme (see section 13.2).

> **Key message**
> Ensure that sponsorship, ownership, terms of reference, scope, processes, roles and responsibilities are clearly defined in the early stages of ITAM implementation.

13.1 IMPLEMENTATION APPROACHES

The implementation of ITAM processes within an organization is an extensive and demanding task. There are many different approaches that can be adopted, and these generally fall into three categories:

- **Internal project** This involves the use of resources from within an organization to implement the ITAM processes. It is the preferred approach if the necessary ITAM skills and knowledge are present and available within the organization. It should involve the use of an approved organizational project methodology (e.g. PRINCE2®).
- **Partnership project** This involves the use of an external partner or partner(s) to assist with the implementation of ITAM processes while maintaining operational control in house. This approach has distinct advantages where there is a shortage of either internal skills or resources.
- **Outsourced project or managed service** This involves contracting an external organization or partner to implement and operate the complete set of activities.

Large decentralized organizations also have another implementation approach to consider, known as a 'coalition of the willing'. In these organizations, ITAM projects often start with a subset of affiliates driving the topic. Others will join later only if convinced by demonstrated benefits or by eventual corporate instruction.

It is important if the complete activity is outsourced that the client still takes ownership of the strategy and makes decisions on information provided. The client still remains accountable for all the assets involved, even when all ITAM activities have been outsourced. Any outsourced contract should be on the basis of criteria that require the supplier to manage the assets effectively, rather than payment based on number of assets managed; otherwise, there is no incentive to dispose of assets not required by the business.

The approach selected by an individual organization will depend upon many factors, including overall cost, the demands for BaU, and the availability of budget, skills and other necessary resources.

13.2 ITAM IMPLEMENTATION COSTS

The costs incurred in implementing ITAM will depend in part on the approach chosen (see section 13.1) and also on other factors such as:

- size, culture and structure of the organization
- level of senior management sponsorship and commitment to ITAM within the organization
- number and types of device in use (e.g. mainframes, servers, desktops, tablets, smartphones, etc.)
- current use of technology and software within the organization
- current state and maturity of the ITAM and ITSM processes within the organization
- ITAM skills, resources and knowledge within the organization
- size, scope and timescale of the proposed project
- tools to be used and the level of automation planned
- degree to which a customized solution is wanted versus the willingness to use existing/available tools and systems that may not meet all perceived requirements.

Key message

The costs associated with the implementation of ITAM processes may seem extensive. However, intelligent exploitation of existing infrastructure, processes and tools will help to contain costs. A good ITAM implementation will typically bring significant financial savings within a year of completion.

ITAM costs should, furthermore, be seen as necessary expenditure to control the many software-related risks faced by an organization.

The main costs will be incurred within the following areas:

- **People** During both the implementation and the subsequent operation stages, people will be required to develop and perform the roles and activities required within ITAM processes, which will include coordinating with other roles and activities. This may require the involvement of not only senior management and project managers but also external partners and consultants where the requisite skills, knowledge and people are in short supply.
- **Tools** Both hardware and software may need to be selected, implemented, configured and tailored to automate aspects of the ITAM processes.
- **Accommodation** There will be accommodation costs for ITAM staff and storage costs for IT assets (e.g. hardware prior to distribution, and when being repaired, refurbished or retired; and physical stores such as for contracts and other documentation).
- **Interfaces** These may need to be developed, using internal or external resources.

■ **Corrective licences** Previously unrecognized liabilities relating to shortfalls in software licences may come to light. The prospect of these costs may deter an organization from starting an ITAM project, but ignoring the liabilities does not make them go away; and a publisher audit may not only identify them but increase the liability considerably. The savings made from effective ITAM processes can potentially more than compensate for the costs of corrective licences.

13.2.1 Ten steps for setting up an ITAM function

Scenario: You work in IT for a small organization which does not have a SAM or ITAM function. Your manager has asked you to set one up, initially to be staffed only by you.

1. **Clarify expectations** Discuss with your manager what is expected, over what time period, and with what resources. How will success be assessed? What is to be your scope: purely licence compliance, purely client-side, or more? Explain your expectations and your intention to follow these ten steps. Put your understanding of expectations in writing.

2. **Start the vertical learning curve** Read this guide. Check out any resources your manager suggests. Join professional ITAM organizations and networking groups, including on LinkedIn. Determine your formal training needs, whether in (generic) ITAM or in detailed topics such as licensing for specific publishers. Plan to attend an ITAM conference as soon as possible. Start ITAM networking.

3. **Study history** Find out whether there have been any earlier attempts to do something similar, and what happened to them. Why did they fail? Have any tools been purchased? Are any in use? What relevant audits (publisher, consultant, external audit, internal audit, etc.) have taken place, and what were the results? (Note: This step may overlap with the next two.)

4. **Determine what IT asset processes, activities and information already exist** What IT asset information is already held, and by whom, for all types of IT assets, including servers and cloud? What information is available about spend by publisher/supplier? (Note: This step may overlap with the next.)

5. **Consult internally** Talk to everyone you can about your new role. Do not promise anything, but find out what they think your top priorities should be, and what value they will get from your work. How could/should you coordinate with them? Ensure that your discussions include people from ITSM, procurement, security, finance and supplier management.

6. **Consult externally** Ask for advice and informal proposals from outsiders about what you should do, and how they might be able to help. Consider your IT resellers, software publishers, tool providers and any IT consulting organizations your department already uses.

7. **Create plans** Outline a tentative long-range plan for the next 2 years, identifying what should be accomplished and when. Develop a detailed plan for the next 6 months with clear deliverables and metrics defined for measuring success.

8. **Agree and sell plans** Agree the short-term plan with your manager. Present the plan to the department. Meet with interested parties both inside and outside the department to get their agreement and buy-in to anything which affects them.

9. **Implement plans** Do it!

10. **Re-assess** Continually review performance against the short-term plan, assessing whether any changes are required, or management intervention needed, to accomplish the planned objectives. Ensure that all processes and improvements are sustainable in the long term. Review and revise CSFs, KPIs and objectives. Keep your manager and all interested parties informed.

13.2.2 Ten steps for setting up a major ITAM programme

Scenario: You work in a small ITAM unit in a medium-sized organization, possibly decentralized and focused on software licence compliance. You have tried in the past to sell an expanded ITAM programme, but without success because management always had other priorities. However, your organization has just been audited by a software publisher with significant underlicensing identified. Management has now decided that it does need much better ITAM processes, especially for licence compliance.

1. **Clarify expectations** Discuss with your manager what they expect you to achieve, over what period, and with what resources. How will success be assessed? What is to be your scope: purely licence compliance or more (e.g. cost savings and improved security)? How will ITAM processes and licence compliance in subsidiaries or affiliates be handled? Explain your expectations and your intention to follow these ten steps. Put your understanding of expectations in writing.

2. **Review where you are on the vertical learning curve** (Re)-read this guide. Review/update your membership of professional ITAM organizations and networking groups, including on LinkedIn. Consider professional qualifications/

certifications for ITAM and related topics, and start on them if needed. Review whether you need to take any formal training in detailed topics, including in particular in licensing for your major spend software publishers. Plan to attend an(other) ITAM conference ASAP. Renew/ start ITAM networking.

3. **Study history** Analyse what when wrong with the failed software publisher audit. Identify underlying causes and determine how to minimize such a risk in future. (Note: This step may overlap with the next two.)

4. **Review the adequacy of existing IT asset information** Are the tools themselves adequate, with only procedural improvements required? Are there multiple overlapping and inconsistent databases, and do responsibilities for updating them need to be clarified? Are new tools needed? (Note: This step may overlap with the next.)

5. **Consult internally** Talk to everyone you can about the major expanded ITAM programme. Do not promise anything, but find out what they think your top priorities should be, and what value they will get from your work. How could/should you coordinate with them? Ensure that your discussions include people from ITSM, procurement, security, finance and supplier management.

6. **Consult externally** Ask for advice and informal proposals from outsiders about what you should do, and how they might be able to help. Consider your IT resellers, software publishers, tool providers and any IT consulting organizations your department already uses.

7. **Create plans** Create a formal business plan for the expanded ITAM role. Ensure that it has a time horizon of at least 2 years, with clear objectives and metrics to demonstrate success. The programme must be designed to be sustainable, with early and continuing

demonstrable benefits in addition to the avoidance of negative publisher audit findings. Create a detailed implementation plan for the first 6–12 months.

8. **Agree and sell plans** Agree the formal business plan and short-term implementation plan with appropriate management. The business plan itself should be agreed by a senior-level executive, and preferably at board level. The level of approval must be high enough to cover any relevant subsidiaries or affiliates. Meet with interested parties both inside and outside the department to present the plans and to get their agreement and buy-in to anything which affects them.

9. **Implement plans** Do it!

10. **Re-assess** Continually review performance against the implementation plan, and consider whether any changes are required, or whether any management intervention is needed to accomplish planned objectives. Keep your manager and all interested parties informed.

13.3 SPECIAL IMPLEMENTATION SITUATION: RE-IMAGING

Small and very small organizations often have huge challenges when they first try to gain control of their IT assets, and of software in particular. These organizations may find that it is more practical to re-image all end-user PCs/devices using standard builds than to go through an exhaustive process of analysing what everyone is using and then creating customized builds intended to meet much of current usage expectations.

SAM/ITAM
and security

14

14 SAM/ITAM and security

14.1 THE SECURITY DRIVER FOR MANAGING SOFTWARE AND OTHER IT ASSETS

Inherently, SAM/ITAM and security management should be among the most tightly integrated disciplines within an organization. Unfortunately, this tends not to be the case. Nonetheless, major developments, mostly driven from the security side, will lead to increased integration and will therefore inevitably have a major impact on the disciplines of SAM and ITAM.

Key message

Security requirements are driving major developments in the management of software, which are in turn starting to have a considerable effect on the disciplines of SAM and ITAM. Improved capabilities for managing software for security purposes also help manage it for most other purposes. SAM/ITAM practitioners need to grasp the opportunities of working together with security, and understand the threats if silo mentalities are not changed.

The need for security automation is the main driver for the security community in looking for better ways of managing software and other IT assets.

The news is increasingly filled with stories about IT security breaches, many of which involve software exposures. 'Good' software can often be exploited through unintended vulnerabilities. Malware itself has progressed from being merely irritating, through being used for ransom, to facilitating large-scale financial and data theft, and also conducting espionage, both commercial and governmental. Perhaps most disturbing is the risk of physical damage and harm, including potential loss of life, as has already been demonstrated with industrial sabotage and the hacking of public utilities such as electricity suppliers. The more automation there is, the greater the exposure, and the risk of various forms of transport being hacked and then controlled is particularly concerning. The exposures in this area are not limited to software, since even hardware is sometimes found to be compromised.

While 'social engineering' lies behind many security breaches, the security risks related to compromised software and hardware will persist even with the most competent and conscientious of personnel. Given the complexity of software and hardware today (including firmware), with the hundreds of thousands of files typically found on many end-user devices, their complex interrelationships, the rate of change for these files, and the lack of interoperable standards for managing software, it has become too demanding for the IT technology and tools of the early 21st century to manage software and its security effectively.

14.2 THE CSCs AND THE NIST CYBERSECURITY FRAMEWORK

There are two major sources of cybersecurity guidance, both of which put IT inventories or asset management as their top priority.

This first of these resulted from developments in the security community, starting in 2008 with the creation of a prioritized list of the 20 most important security controls which help in the prevention of security breaches, and their prompt identification and effective mitigation if breaches do occur. These are sometimes referred to as the SANS critical security controls, CSCs or CIS controls (see Further information for more details and to obtain current information about the CSCs).

As described on the CIS website:

'The CIS Critical Security Controls (CIS Controls) are a concise, prioritized set of cyber practices created to stop today's most pervasive and dangerous cyber attacks. The CIS Controls are developed, refined and validated by a community of leading experts from around the world. Organizations that apply just the first five CIS Controls can reduce their risk of cyber attack by around 85 percent. Implementing all 20 CIS Controls increases the risk reduction to around 94 percent.' (CIS, 2017)

The highest priority controls in this list are all SAM/ITAM controls. The top three are:

- **CSC1** Inventory of Authorized and Unauthorized Devices
- **CSC2** Inventory of Authorized and Unauthorized Software
- **CSC3** Secure Configurations for Hardware and Software on Mobile Devices, Laptops, Workstations and Servers.

The first two CSCs are the most fundamental of SAM/ITAM inventories. The need to clearly identify the authorization status of all assets, at a detailed level, currently cannot be met by most SAM/ITAM

tools. Furthermore, security authorizations may be structured differently from financial, technical or managerial authorizations.

The third CSC is also a SAM/ITAM control, but less obvious. Another way of stating the control is that an organization should not distribute hardware or software unless it is securely configured (e.g. do not distribute web browsers with insecure configurations, and do not distribute software with default user IDs and passwords).

Note that in 2016 these controls were also published by the European Telecommunications Standards Institute (ETSI) (CIS, 2016).

The second source of cybersecurity guidance to cite is the Cybersecurity Framework issued by the US National Institute for Standards and Technology on 12 February 2014 (NIST, 2014) and mandated for US federal agencies in a US presidential executive order on 11 May 2017 (White House, 2017). The NIST Cybersecurity Framework specifies asset management as the first requirement of the framework core.

14.3 THE CSCs AND PERSONAL DATA PROTECTION

The protection of personal data from unauthorized access and use has become exceptionally important in many jurisdictions, such as the EU with its General Data Protection Regulation which comes into effect in 2018. General security controls are a necessary part of personal data protection. It is useful to note that the State of California, which has a law requiring notification of personal data breaches, has issued a specific recommendation for organizations that they: 'Adopt the Center for Internet Security's Critical Security Controls as the start of a comprehensive information security program, since not doing so would be indicative of a failure to provide reasonable security' (California, State of, 2016). California's Assistant Attorney General, in a discussion about this, cited the first two controls (inventories of hardware and software) and stated that this was also the place to inventory personal data held (CIS, New America, 2017).

14.4 THE RELATIONSHIPS AND DISCONNECTS BETWEEN SAM/ITAM AND SECURITY

Inherently, both SAM/ITAM and security disciplines are concerned with the detailed management of software and other IT assets. Since it is not possible to manage what is not known, both disciplines therefore require detailed knowledge about IT assets. However, in practice to-date the two disciplines seldom use the same databases or tools for their respective purposes. Some of the reasons for this are:

■ SAM generally focuses on asset identification for the purposes of software licence compliance, and this is usually at the product level at which licensing requirements are determined. Security is generally concerned with a more detailed level of information (e.g. ensuring that products have all necessary security patches).

■ Security will focus on whether devices connected to the network are properly authorized, with a need for quick response if unauthorized devices are detected. SAM may not focus on devices except at periodic intervals when they may be checked for licensing purposes.

■ Security will be concerned about whether any file is malware or has been tampered with, which is generally not a SAM concern. Dealing with this issue requires an extreme level of detail and extreme volumes of information. In most

situations this can only be handled on a limited basis (i.e. incompletely) and is where there is a particular need for security automation.

■ SAM includes significant focus on 'bean-counting' (i.e. determining the usage of specific software or of software access rights). This is not an issue for security.

Even though both disciplines are concerned with the detailed management of software, they tend not to integrate their efforts because of these different sets of requirements. Both being represented on the change management committee is often the best approach for improving their cooperation and integration.

14.5 THE SOFTWARE IDENTIFICATION TAG AND SECURITY

14.5.1 Common data requirements for ITAM and security

Despite what was stated in the previous paragraph, SAM/ITAM and security management have some similar requirements that are starting to be met by the ISO software identification (SWID) tag standard. The discussion below specifically addresses how the SWID tag addresses security requirements while also addressing those for SAM/ITAM (see section D.2 for more detail).

The importance of SWID tags for security automation is reflected in their endorsement by major organizations. For example, the US Department of Defense (DoD) IT Standards Registry now lists SWID tags, as defined in ISO/IEC 19770-2, as mandatory (Defense Standardization Program). The US National Institute for Standards and Technology has a number of publications relating to

SWID tags and security (use search on nist.gov). The Trusted Computing Group (2015) also has a publication relating to the their use.

Several pieces of information that are required for both asset management and security can be provided by the SWID tag, namely:

■ **An authoritative list of software products installed on a computing device** This means that we know the publisher of each software item (product, patch, driver, etc.), we can identify every product installed on a device, and we have a unique ID that represents a specific version of a specific software product. (Third-party application recognition libraries take a best guess at recognition, based on artefacts discovered on a device, whereas the SWID tag can provide precise data that the users can trust.)

■ **Definition of the files that make up each software product** This means that we can identify exactly which files on a device belong to a specific software item. The approach within the SWID tag standard allows specifying a list of files (payload) that includes a cryptographically strong hash for each file. The SWID tag itself being digitally signed means we can identify any files on a computing device that have been modified since their originally distribution.

■ **Relationships between the software items installed** This means that we can identify relationships between software items, such as individual software components that have been distributed as a suite, or patches that are related to one or more software items installed on a device. This approach will allow software publishers to include links that show which software items are related to each other (Link) and the relationship (rel) between them.

With this type of data, management systems can provide automation for SAM/ITAM and security. Furthermore, using the SWID tag provides the following additional benefits for data:

■ normalization (enabling data on a device and across devices and tools to be compared)
■ structure (enabling different tools and management systems to use the exact same data).

14.5.2 SWID tags and malware scanners

Malware scanners typically use some form of reputation score for any given executable file in order to distinguish a genuine file, created by a commercial publisher, from a malicious program. This is generally accomplished by checking each executable file against a list of commercial files that have been installed on a wide range of machines in the wider community and known not to have been the source of malicious behaviour.

Unfortunately, malware scanners have a recognition problem with new, genuine software. When a commercial publisher releases a new software update or patch, the new files in that new release do not yet have a reputation score. This leads to the first adopters of the new software receiving a false positive that the software may not be distributed from a known and trusted publisher.

SWID tags that include the file manifest (payload) solve this problem since the hash data which the malware scanners require is included with the SWID tag.

14.5.3 SWID tags, vulnerability identification, and patching

The US and other countries provide support to collect and collate vulnerability information from multiple sources in order to help all organizations improve the security of their computing environments. In the US, this is done through the use of the Security Content Automation Protocol (SCAP), which is managed primarily by NIST. Much of this data is made public through the National Vulnerability Database (NVD).

Because vulnerability and remediation processes come from multiple sources, NIST attempted to create a normalized naming structure for software and hardware that is called the common platform enumeration (CPE). Unfortunately, due to the fact that the normalization effort for software products is not being driven by the software publishers, the CPE approach has many of the same problems as those identified in the discovery tool category (see section 11.4.3). To add to the complications, the CPE data is not normalized and is updated by many people, who take different approaches to naming.

This means that there is a very large set of incredibly useful data in the NVD and SCAP databases that is not being utilized to its full potential. A number of publishers utilize these data sources, but it involves them spending significant resources linking data from the NVD and SCAP databases with the actual patches, software and configuration details that are provided.

If you review the NVD system, you will also find that there are often numerous manual steps involved in the overall effort to:

■ identify whether a patch is appropriate for a particular device
■ find the patch
■ download the patch
■ install the patch.

This process is very different for a publisher who uses SWID tags. Such usage means that:

■ there are normalized names for both the software as well as all patches, so that no matter where the information about a vulnerability comes from, exactly the same data is used by all cybersecurity researchers and environments
■ a simple inventory is sufficient to identify whether a patch is needed and/or installed, since patches identify and enumerate every software item to which they apply
■ systems which utilize NVD and SCAP data can automatically and reliably associate that data with the software on a device through the SWID tag data.

In short, the vulnerability management lifecycle that every software product goes through is much more automated and accurate using SWID tags than with the patchwork legacy approach.

Software publisher licence compliance audits

15

15 Software publisher licence compliance audits

Software publisher audits are the most common cause of SAM/ITAM initiatives, plans or programmes. However, it is better and more efficient to proactively plan the establishment of SAM/ITAM processes and activities than to hastily respond to an adverse compliance audit by a specific software publisher. A planned programme is able to meet the interests of the organization and satisfy the needs of all software publishers.

SAM/ITAM involves collecting inventory, financial and entitlement data to manage IT assets throughout their lifecycles. End-user organizations are spending about 8 per cent of revenue on their IT assets annually, and according to Forrester Research (2015), only 17 per cent of organizations have full visibility into the software installed across their desktop environments. Given the sums involved, it is difficult to understand why more organizations do not proactively manage that spend.

Key outcomes from a successful SAM/ITAM programme are reduced cost and reduced risk resulting from the identification and elimination of unlicensed software, and from licence optimization. If the key outcomes are so commonly achieved, why do more end-user organizations not have SAM/ITAM programmes?

Publisher audits are likely both to increase in frequency and to extend to smaller end-user organizations as publisher audit processes become more efficient and better at identifying the 'red flags' that indicate likely underlicensing.

Software publisher audit action checklist

The organization should have a well-defined procedure to follow when a software publisher audit notification is received. This procedure should be considered even for 'friendly' reviews which are not formally audits but which may have the same unplanned financial impact. Such reviews should be assessed on a case-by-case basis, because they can give benefits such as lower pricing, but they may not be as friendly as promoted.

Major steps which should be considered are:

- **Involve senior management** Once an audit notice is received, or even suggested, ensure that senior management is immediately notified.
- **Review publisher audit rights** Review the end-user licence agreement (EULA) or contract for the publisher. Is the publisher permitted by agreement to do the audit (and to do it now)?
- **Assess underlicensing exposure** Immediately start assessing what your licensing exposure may be. Create (or check existing) inventory of your installed software for that publisher and start reviewing your licence entitlements. Make sure the publisher provides you with a full list of your entitlements, including for organizations you acquired that may be within the scope of this audit. Ensure that you have an independent check on issues requiring licensing expertise.

■ **Consider obtaining professional help** If it appears that the underlicensing exposure may be significant, you may need a competent external adviser, both from a licensing perspective and also for dealing with the audit itself.

■ **Find out about the experience of others** Speak to your peers who may have been audited by the same publisher. How did they resolve it? If all else fails, seek input from experts.

■ **Manage contacts with the publisher** During the entire process, ensure that you limit who is authorized to speak to the publisher. Publishers are always looking for more information to support their findings; this is not the time to speak out of turn or rush a response.

■ **Stay calm** Use the information you learned and the data you collected to your benefit. Does your installation information match the publisher's? Research the methodology used by the publisher; make sure you understand it and, if not, ask questions. Do not be intimidated. Auditors are fallible; they can make major mistakes.

■ **Have clarity at exit** At the conclusion of the audit, make sure there is a clear understanding of your entitlements moving forward, and of the next audit date. Seek an audit close letter confirming these details and anything else that may have been agreed.

It is also important to know what may cause a publisher software audit, and to try to establish the likely reason for each specific audit announced. First and foremost, many publishers are starting to re-audit customers at regular frequencies, generally every 2–3 years, probably influenced by any prior history of underlicensing. Publishers also monitor information which can provide red flags about possible underlicensing to drive audit activity. For example, has there been merger or acquisition activity, major growth or geographic expansion? Have there been changes in purchasing levels, and reduction or cancellation of support/maintenance? Has the head of IT recently changed? If so, the time of change might be seen as a good opportunity for the new management to clean up the organization. In some publishers the licence compliance function is closely linked to the sales function, so there might be a perception of a direct audit linkage. (It can be useful to understand exactly where the publisher's audit function reports vis-à-vis the sales function, and how significant its revenue targets are compared with regular sales targets.) Audits might also happen if there are suggestions that an organization may be moving away from a publisher's software.

> **Key message**
> Implementing a SAM/ITAM project will probably impact your licence purchasing patterns. This in turn will likely trigger at least one publisher audit. Ensure that one of the early deliverables of a SAM/ITAM project is a well-developed procedure for responding to these.

Software audits do not need to be adversarial; neither do they need to be one-sided, favouring the publisher. Good data, good processes and good SAM practices are the main way of ensuring that only what is being used is being paid for.

Establishment of a SAM/ITAM programme is not the only possible outcome of a negative audit experience. Other typical types of response are:

1. Do nothing, possibly because of being overwhelmed by other issues. This is common. The root causes of licence non-compliance will persist, and the publisher will be back for another audit in 2–3 years. Other publishers will also probably learn about the customer and likewise conduct audits. However, after a number of negative licence compliance audit experiences, SAM/ITAM may finally be seen as the necessary solution.

2. Do nothing because of a considered management decision. Rather than invest in SAM and other IT management systems, simply accept that there will be regular publisher audits on which management will rely for achieving licence compliance. Use audits to negotiate new agreements with reduced pricing, wherever possible.

3. Implement SAM/ITAM to get the situation under control and avoid similar issues in the future. If you can gain benefits in addition to licence compliance, that is a plus. But the main driver is licence compliance and the avoidance of the negative impact of publisher audits.

4. Establish provisions for potential audit licence compliance costs, to avoid major unexpected financial impacts. Combine this approach with (2) or (3). The provision with (3) will be less than with (2). For (3), it will be primarily to cover audits from minor publishers not covered (yet) in detail by SAM/ITAM.

Appendix A: Software
industry supply chain

A

Appendix A: Software industry supply chain

Many organizations and players are involved in the sale and distribution of software, with the user organization at the end of a long and sometimes complex chain, as depicted in Figure A.1. The onus is on the user organization to ensure that the software provided is genuine. The following are the roles of the main players within the software industry:

- **Software publishers** Responsible for providing quality software that is fit for purpose, together with all licensing information necessary for the use of the software. Software is the intellectual property of the publisher; all that the user purchases is a licence to use it.

- **Original equipment manufacturers (OEMs)** Install software on their hardware and sell it on as a package. The licence for OEM software is typically from the OEM rather than the software publisher (the main exception to that general rule). As a result, OEM licences are usually contractually bound to the hardware with which they are sold, and are not transferable to other machines.

- **Distributors** Do not usually deal directly with end-customers, but only with software publishers and resellers. They deal in very high volumes of software of low-volume types (e.g. retail products, low-volume programmes and OEM products). Some counterfeit products have entered the supply channel via (smaller) distributors.

- **Resellers** Deal directly with end-customers for most levels of software purchasing (e.g. retail, OEM, and low- and high-volume programmes). Counterfeit products have entered the supply channel via smaller resellers. Some software publishers have authorized resellers, with whom the risk of buying counterfeit products should be minimized.

- **Advisers** Assist customers in placing orders, but the contractual relationships are directly between the customer and the software publisher, which pays a fee to the adviser. Many resellers also offer advisory services.

- **End-user organization** The organization that ultimately purchases the licences, and is responsible for ensuring that genuine proof of licence is received for all purchases made.

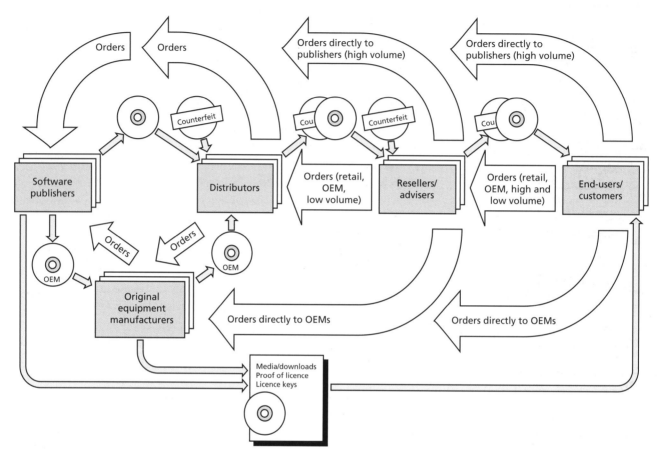

Figure A.1 The software industry supply chain

Note that Figure A.1 is simplified and focuses on media delivered physically. Not all channels are shown, nor all possibilities for ordering or delivering, or for the introduction of counterfeit product.

Appendix B: Software licensing overview

B

Appendix B: Software licensing overview

Note: The information in this guide, and in this appendix in particular, does not constitute legal advice. Each organization needs to determine its own situation with respect to the laws relevant to itself, including contract law, and relevant licensing terms and conditions. The information given in this guide is intended to provide background context for such specific determinations by individual organizations.

Software licensing is complex, and compliance with all its terms and conditions requires in-depth knowledge. An organization needs to assign the responsibility for understanding licensing to specific individuals, and then ensure that they have the necessary training (initial and ongoing) to master the area. It is also advisable to have a periodic independent check on licensing requirements, regardless of the level of expertise of the individual with primary responsibility.

This guide is not a substitute for an organization understanding its own licensing terms and conditions. However, this appendix gives a flavour of the complexity that can be found in software licensing. All comments within it are generic, and may not correspond to the specific terms and conditions of particular software.

B.1 WHEN LICENCES ARE REQUIRED

Software licences are rights to use software, with certain terms and conditions attached, and are one of the main issues addressed by SAM/ITAM. These rights to use software are separate from the legal rights to the software itself, which are normally

kept by the software publisher or other third party. Licences may be paid for or 'free', subject to special terms and conditions. Even 'open-source' software normally has a licence, although payment may not be required.

Licences are normally required whenever externally sourced software is 'used', which will typically be defined either as being installed or executed on a machine, even if installed elsewhere (e.g. a server). They may also be defined in 'enterprise' terms, such as number of workstations or employees, in which case a licence is required for each qualifying unit or individual regardless of actual 'usage'.

Even with commercial software, there are several situations where paid licences may not be required, depending on specific contractual conditions. These situations are often not understood and, as a result, organizations may purchase licences they do not need. These situations may include workstations used for dedicated training purposes (with limits on numbers), copies used for evaluation purposes (with conditions on how they are used and for how long) and copies used for distribution purposes. Likewise, there can be 'runtime' versions of some software, which do not require separate paid licences. (It may be difficult to distinguish between installed runtime and non-runtime versions of such software.)

Back-ups are problematic legally. Many software contracts allow for only one back-up copy for archival purposes, contrary to good IT practice for making back-ups. However, it is unlikely that a software publisher would make an issue of this, or that a court would uphold it if taken that far. The critical issue is that the copies should be purely for back-up purposes, with no more copies ever being used (installed or executed) than are licensed. The situation for 'hot' back-ups is different, because in these cases the back-up software is installed. Reference must be made to specific licence terms and conditions in these cases.

B.2 LICENCES AND ENTITLEMENTS

The terms 'licence' and 'entitlement' are often used interchangeably, and also in phrases such as 'proof of licence' and 'effective licence'.

This publication uses these and related terms in the following senses in the context of software licensing:

- **Licence** This is the formally documented right to use software, with its associated terms and conditions. It is transactional (i.e. it is obtained at a specific time; for example, as the result of a commercial sales transaction or some other action such as agreeing to a 'click-through' licence before downloading or running software). It may be for a full product, or it may be usable only in combination with another licence (see, for example, section B.3.3).
- **Effective licence** This is the right to use a specific full software product, with its associated terms and conditions, separate from the formal licence(s). It potentially consolidates the use rights, terms and conditions of multiple underlying licences. It is not transactional, but represents information consolidated from one or more licensing transactions. It may change over time (e.g. depending on the latest software product that has been released if an underlying licence gives software upgrade rights).

- **Entitlement** This is the right to use specific software, with its associated terms and conditions, separate from the formal licence(s). 'Entitlement' may be used in two different senses:
  - the use rights, terms and conditions associated with a specific licence
  - the use rights, terms and conditions associated with a combination of licences (i.e. an effective licence).

  'Entitlement' is more generally understood in the second sense (i.e. as a synonym for effective licence).
- **Proof of licence** This is documentary evidence of a licence; for example, via authenticated licence confirmations (see section B.8 for a more detailed discussion).
- **Proof of entitlement** This term conflates 'proof of licence' with 'proof' of the calculations of any effective licences resulting from those underlying licences. To avoid misunderstandings this publication does not use this term, because 'proof' of effective licences is usually based on analysis, and not on documentary evidence that could be authenticated.

B.3 BASIC TYPES OF LICENCE

B.3.1 Duration

The following licence types are based on duration:

- **Perpetual** Historically, most licences sold have been perpetual (i.e. the use rights are permanent after purchase).
- **Subscription or rental** Can be used for a specific period of time, which can vary from days to years; or for a specified number of uses, however defined. These licences may or may not include upgrade rights.

■ **Temporary** Other cases of time-limited licences (e.g. pending full payment or receipt of proof of licence).

B.3.2 Measure of usage

Usage can be based on:

■ **Per copy used, by workstation/seat/device or named user** Historically, most licences have been sold on a per-copy-used basis; several different units of measurement are possible. Sometimes many users are allowed per licence. Note that licensing is sometimes based on unit counts other than PCs. For example, printer counts are important in several licensing schemes (e.g. for fonts where there may be a limit on the number of printers that can download the fonts per licence, and for some networking software node counts). Likewise, cloud computing and mobile devices (e.g. smartphones and tablets) have licensing requirements that may not be recognized by many 'traditional' approaches to licence management based on PCs.

■ **Concurrent usage** Allows a specified number of users to connect simultaneously to a software application. This is a commonly understood licensing approach, and there are many software products to help monitor and control concurrent usage. However, such licences are becoming less common.

■ **Per processor, per core or per server speed** Server licences are often linked to the number of processors or, increasingly, of physical or virtual cores (i.e. independent processing units in a processor). Likewise, especially for larger computers, licences may be linked to the speed or power of the server on which they are run.

■ **Client/server access licences** Unlike most licences, these do not correspond to physical installations or use of software, and are frequently misunderstood. CALs give a client device the right to access a server package, regardless of whether there is client software associated with it. The detailed terms and conditions for such licences prohibit software 'tricks' to combine multiple clients into a single channel for licensing purposes.

■ **Enterprise or site** Increasingly, licences are being sold on an enterprise or site basis that requires just a count of qualifying entities (usually workstations or employees). This is easier for administration purposes, especially in organizations with limited SAM capabilities. Nonetheless, people who do not understand the contractual definition of the enterprise may try to apply 'per copy' counting rules instead. A further complication is that qualifying workstations or employees/contractors may not be easy to identify.

■ **Other complexities** Other, more complex situations also exist with regard to licensing and the use of techniques such as multiplexing, clustering, virtualization, shared services, 'thin clients', roaming services and cloud computing. These situations can be expensive and need careful management on a case-by-case basis.

B.3.3 Upgrades

Many types of upgrade are available, each with detailed conditions as to what is acceptable as a basis for the upgrade. A common problem is the purchase of upgrade licences for which there are no qualifying underlying licences (e.g. maintenance may have been purchased without an underlying product being owned, in which case the licences are invalid for use). Typical upgrades include:

- **Version upgrades** A later release of the same product
- **Product upgrades** Changes within a product family (e.g. a partial suite of products being upgraded to a more extensive suite of the same product family)
- **Competitive upgrades** Based on competitive products
- **Language upgrades** Allow the use of a more expensive product with different/additional language capabilities
- **Upgrade insurance** Many software publishers offer upgrade 'insurance' under a variety of names (e.g. for maintenance). They allow the purchasers to use any upgrades that are released during the period of the insurance. A common problem is that organizations forget the upgrade rights they purchased with this insurance because they do not perform the physical upgrade during the same time period. They then purchase the upgrades again later when the physical upgrade is performed
- **Technology guarantees** Limited-duration upgrade rights that a software publisher may grant to purchasers of one version of software when a new version is expected but not yet released. It is important to note these rights when they are issued, as they may be difficult to determine retrospectively.

B.3.4 End-user type

The following licences are based on the types of user:

- **Commercial nature (retail, commercial, governmental, not-for-profit and academic)** There is a hierarchy of pricing levels for different types of organizations, with retail purchasers and commercial organizations paying the most and academic users paying the least. The risk is that less expensive licences are purchased in situations that do not qualify, such as academic licences for commercial purposes.
- **Commercial versus personal** Some licences charge for commercial use but not personal use. This is common with some shareware/freeware packages.

B.3.5 Licence management responsibility

Responsibility for managing licences is based on the following categories:

- **Customer-managed usage (CMU)** Most licences require customer management or oversight, and that is the focus of this guide.
- **Publisher-managed usage (PMU)** Falls into two broad categories:
  - For software run on the vendor's systems (e.g. a cloud service provider), the vendor typically measures the usage and reports it to the customer, together with related billings
  - For software run on the customer's own hardware, some software publishers have technical licence management products. These may rely, for example, on licence servers that control the number of users able to use the software.

For both categories it is still advisable for the end-user (or customer) to monitor, and periodically validate, publisher usage figures, both as a check on the correctness of publisher measurements, and to facilitate strategic planning.

B.3.6 Other

Other types of licence include:

- **Suite** A group of applications sold together. The terms of the licence normally preclude the individual applications being separated and used individually on separate devices, or by different users simultaneously.

■ **Secondary or portable use** Provides for the use of software either by secondary users or in a secondary location; for example, the ability to use one licence on a desktop and a laptop, or on a work computer and a home computer. Secondary use rights may come with the main licence, or may be sold separately.

■ **Locked licence** Requires an activation key and is not readily copied or moved.

■ **Token-activated** Uses a dongle or security device to restrict usage.

■ **Serialized licence** Identifiable by a unique serial number; it is therefore easier to check authenticity.

B.4 TYPES OF LICENCE BY SALES CHANNEL

There are frequently differences in licence terms and conditions depending on the sales channel. For example:

■ **Original equipment manufacturers (OEMs)** These often have their own licensing terms for software that they supply together with equipment. One of the most significant conditions attached to such software is that it can be used only on the original equipment. If the equipment is replaced, the software cannot be moved to a new machine (although any upgrades used may be movable). The EULA for OEM software is normally between the equipment manufacturer and the end-user, and not between the software publisher and the end-user.

■ **Retail** Software sold in retail packaging is the closest to a typical hardware product in terms of physical characteristics. It is also the most expensive, and maintaining the proof of licence is the most onerous for this type of product.

■ **Low volume** There are low-volume methods of purchasing software licences that do not require the signing of a contract with the software publisher, but that usually require user registration. Media may have to be purchased separately. There may be some limited audit rights associated with such licences.

■ **High volume** The high-volume methods of purchasing software licences generally require a signed contract with the software publisher. There are several levels of contract and/or pricing. This type of contract typically gives the software publisher significant audit rights.

■ **Service provider** Software is increasingly being made available through hosting organizations or cloud service providers. This is normally on a subscription or other temporary rights basis.

■ **Solution provider** Software, and sometimes hardware from multiple publishers and vendors, may be bundled by a 'solution provider' as a turn-key package (i.e. a complete package of all software needed). These range from small packages to major enterprise resource planning (ERP) systems. These bundled licences need to be controlled as part of SAM.

■ **Shareware, freeware and public domain software** Tend to be distributed via the internet rather than through commercial resellers. There may be many such packages in use within an organization (e.g. zipping utilities). They should be subject to the same controls as software procured from major software publishers:

● **Shareware** Users are encouraged to copy the program for preview purposes. If the user intends to keep using it then a licence fee must be paid to the developer.

- **Freeware** No licence fee is paid but these programs still come with a licence agreement that could potentially be violated (see also 'open-source' below).
- **Public domain** Needs to be clearly marked as such, and means the copyright holder has relinquished all rights to the software so it can be freely copied, modified, enhanced, etc.

■ **Open-source** A version of freeware that provides source code. There are many variants of open-source licences, some of which require subsequent modifications to be made publicly available as well. The licences themselves are free, but there may be charges for media and distribution, and commercial support contracts are common.

B.5 LICENSING, LIABILITY AND OUTSOURCING

The user of licensed software is normally liable to the licensor of that software for non-compliance with contractual terms and conditions (when software licences have been obtained) and for violation of copyright and other laws relating to that software (when the software is being used without licences). When an organization manages its own software and licensing, it clearly has a direct liability to the software licensor, which is usually the software publisher.

> **Key message**
>
> Liability for software licence non-compliance cannot be outsourced.

The issue of liability when outsourcing, however, is often misunderstood. In particular, there is a common misperception that any outsourcing related to software (including for 'full' SAM) can result in the outsourcing organization taking on the liabilities concerning the use of that software. In general, this is untrue. More specifically, while services can be outsourced, liability associated with those services generally cannot be transferred unless clearly agreed by the other parties involved (in particular the licensor and the outsourcer). The best that could be expected in most situations is to obtain an indemnity from the outsourcer covering such liabilities. Outsourcers are unlikely to agree to significant indemnities in this respect, if at all, without major provisions for ensuring control over software licensing.

Some unexpected software licensing liabilities can occur in non-software outsourcing that are not necessarily well understood; for example, the use of third-party suppliers for hardware (e.g. Infrastructure as a Service (IaaS) or Platform as a Service (PaaS) from cloud service providers, or more traditional hosted data centre services). Major software exposure could result if the provider increases the number of server cores to improve response time, but the customer does not recognize the impact on per-core licence costs.

The message here is that an organization needs to be aware of, and in control of, its liability with respect to software licensing, regardless of whether or not any of its services are outsourced.

B.6 PIRATED AND COUNTERFEIT SOFTWARE

Pirated software is legitimate software that is intentionally installed beyond what is permitted by its licensing terms and conditions. (The term 'pirating' is sometimes used to refer to all underlicensing, but it more correctly implies underlicensing with intent, or at least serious negligence.) An example of pirated software is 'hard-disk loading', whereby a dealer may load unlicensed copies of legitimate software onto the machines it sells. With this and other types of pirated software, none of the materials supplied purport to have come from the software publisher. End-user organizations themselves can also pirate software, because much software is now downloaded and often relies only on registration keys that may be improperly shared. However, publishers are increasingly requiring online registration to limit the opportunity for this type of abuse.

Counterfeit software is non-genuine software that appears to be genuine, including its related proof-of-licence materials. It typically includes code from genuine software, but has modifications (e.g. to bypass licensing restrictions and/or add malware). Purchasing counterfeit software is commonly viewed as a trivial risk. However, for comparison purposes, the Office for Economic Co-operation and Development (OECD) published a report in 2017 stating that, on average, '6.5% of global trade in information and communication technology (ICT) goods is in counterfeit products, according to analysis of 2013 customs data' (OECD, 2017). These primarily concern hardware products, but a similar caution also applies to software, and indeed the risk for software is probably significantly larger because of the ease of duplication and distribution.

There is a higher risk of purchasing counterfeit software than many organizations realize, especially for retail products purchased from resellers. This is because of the sophistication of counterfeiters, and the lack of attention that some resellers and end-user organizations pay to this issue. The risks of using counterfeit software include the following:

- not being licensed for the software being used
- loss of money spent on the counterfeit software (rather than an apparent saving)
- being in violation of copyright and trademark legislation through possession of the counterfeit products.

The main factors for increased risk of counterfeit software are:

- **Status of suppliers and source of product** Some software publishers sell software directly or through authorized resellers. There is no real risk of purchasing counterfeit products from the publisher, and the risk from an authorized reseller is significantly reduced. A reseller with no special status, selling goods that purport to come from the 'grey market' (i.e. produced for a different marketing area from where it is being sold), may involve significantly more risk. 'Grey market' products in particular are at high risk of being counterfeit, because this is a common way for a reseller to explain the low cost of counterfeit products.

- **Length of distribution chain** Collateral or proof of licence received directly from a software publisher is the best guarantee of authenticity. The more tiers there are in the distribution channel between the software publisher and the end-customer, the greater the risk of counterfeit product entering the chain.

- **Size of reseller** Larger resellers are usually more established and have more to lose if caught selling counterfeit products. They should take extra measures to ensure they are dealing only with genuine products. Smaller resellers may be more susceptible to selling counterfeit software, knowingly or unknowingly.

■ **Geographical location** If the transaction is based in a country with less stringent copyright/trademark laws or enforcement, the risk of counterfeit software increases.

These risk factors are for awareness only; they are not absolute. There are small resellers at the end of long distribution chains, based in countries with weak intellectual property protection, but selling genuine products. Nevertheless, the buyer has a particular duty of care to ensure that the product it is buying is genuine even though there are increased risk factors.

Definitive guidance about how to identify counterfeits is beyond the scope of this publication. However, the following steps are recommended:

■ Assess the likelihood of counterfeit product based on the risk factors involved (see above).

■ Be knowledgeable about each software publisher's security features designed to fight counterfeiting. Descriptions of these may be found on software publishers' websites.

■ Make it clear to your resellers in advance that you will check for the authenticity of the product supplied, especially if the price looks particularly low.

■ Review all software collateral received for the relevant security features, with a degree of attention corresponding to the risk factors involved.

■ Refer to the software publisher directly in cases of doubt.

B.7 PHYSICAL MANAGEMENT OF SOFTWARE LICENCES

A number of challenges are associated with the physical management of licences:

■ **Varied physical characteristics** The types of collateral that can constitute proof of licence have a wide variety of forms and storage characteristics.

■ **High risk of loss** Affects many types of proof of licence, especially in decentralized environments.

■ **Risk of holding counterfeit licences** See section B.6.

■ **Implementing an effective records management system** There need to be separate systems for storage (physical and electronic) and for recording what is in storage (similar to the difference between a warehouse and the stock control records for the warehouse).

■ **Linking multiple licences to determine effective licences** One current effective licence (or entitlement) may require many prior purchases. For example, a single effective licence may be the result of a series of upgrades on an earlier product, and the documentation needs to be retained and linked to show how they build on each other. There is an associated risk of double-counting of licences (i.e. that all these documents will be considered as individual licences and totalled, rather than considered together as contractually required). There is also a risk of double-counting licences when there are multiple forms of support (e.g. certificates of authenticity (COAs) and invoices).

B.8 CONTRACTUAL DOCUMENTATION AND PROOF OF LICENCE

For software licences purchased under volume-licensing programmes (which generally have the best pricing), the full set of contractual documentation often consists of a complex set of documents, some electronic and some physical, which constitute the full set of contractual documentation. Sometimes it includes terms and conditions that may change over time and are primarily accessible via the internet. It is generally only for 'retail' type software licences that a single contractual document, such as a EULA, may exist.

'Proof of licence' is what a court will accept as proof of a legal entity having a licence. However, it should rarely be necessary to resort to court. Because each software publisher in general states the requirements for its proof of licence, no hard and fast rules can be given here. Generally proof of licence requires some form of evidence directly from the software publisher. Evidence of payments made to a reseller, or licence confirmations produced by a reseller, will not usually constitute acceptable proof of licence. The main types of evidence for having a licence include the following, of which the first three are usually the most important:

■ Electronic licence confirmation documents from software publishers held on controlled-access websites.
■ Printed licence confirmation documents from software publishers (with security features).
■ COAs that are typically engraved, or with other security features. These may be:
  ● labels glued onto equipment
  ● labels printed or glued on retail boxes
  ● loose pieces of paper
  ● pieces of paper pasted onto manual covers.
  Although certificates of authenticity are important, back-up collateral is often required, because under some circumstances a COA may be attached to an illegal/counterfeit copy (e.g. an unlabelled COA for a less expensive product repackaged with a counterfeit, more expensive product).
■ Purchasing records or analyses provided by software publishers, plus proof of payment.
■ Volume purchasing contracts.

■ Free-standing letters or other documentation from software publishers confirming a grant of licences.
■ Invoices from resellers, plus proof of payment.
■ Media (CDs, disks, DVDs, plus associated 'jewel case' boxes often with serial numbers, especially for retail products).
■ Documentation (especially for older retail products).
■ Sales documentation (e.g. product brochures). It may be desirable to keep copies of this to clarify the licences that are included with specific packaged products (e.g. OEM products). The descriptions given on invoices in such cases are often insufficient to clarify what licences are included. In the absence of other stronger documentation, this may be important in helping to establish licence ownership.

Example of contractual definition of proof-of-volume licences

'This agreement, the applicable enrolment, the enrolled affiliate's order confirmation, and any documentation evidencing transfers of perpetual licences, together with proof of payment, will be the enrolled affiliate's evidence of all licences obtained under an enrolment.'

A 'licence confirmation' document produced by a reseller, sometimes with its own security features, is not usually an acceptable proof of licence, regardless of how impressive it may seem. Many resellers have produced such documents for a number of reasons, such as the delays in customers getting software publisher confirmations and the consolidation of reporting that may occur in software publisher confirmations. However, they are not proof of licence, and may create significant legal and financial exposures.

Check with the software publisher directly about what documentation it requires you to retain. You may want to negotiate on this if you feel the administrative tasks would be onerous. Any such 'special dispensations' should be obtained from the publisher in writing.

B.8.1 Physical characteristics

Although some types of proof of licence are easy to store in traditional filing systems, particularly the printed 'volume-licensing confirmations', the majority are more difficult to store. The following are some particular examples:

- **OEM operating system licences** Most COAs are now physically fixed to a PC, and cannot be removed without effectively destroying them. There is no option for separate physical storage of this document, and it can be controlled only in a database. Barcode readers may be used to capture the relevant information.
- **Electronic confirmations** Many software publishers' volume licence confirmation documents now are purely electronic. Although the online copy is definitive it is prudent to print a copy and treat the printout as if it were a hard-copy original licence confirmation for ease of reference and as back-up for the electronic online version.
- **Media** Primarily concerns older software, or where current licences are based on upgrades from older licences where media formed part of the proof of licence. For example, a company may have purchased large quantities of software via a non-volume channel, so there is a CD to keep with each. There may have been successive upgrades, including to competitive products, but the original CD is still part of the proof of original licence on which all successive upgrades are based.

- **Manuals** Also primarily concerns older software, especially where the COAs were pasted onto manual covers. If the manuals were given to end-users, the certificates were likely to be lost. However, keeping them centrally in manual form was also problematic. One solution practised by some organizations was to rip off and store the covers with their certificates, and throw away the manuals.

If you have a large quantity of bulky support collateral for early licences, such as CDs, it is worth asking the software publisher of your latest licences if it will accept in writing as valid a certificate of destruction from a recognized destruction agent, citing the relevant details of the materials destroyed. However, some software publishers have refused to allow the destruction of CDs even though they were very old.

B.8.2 High risk of loss

There is a high risk of loss of physical licences, especially in decentralized environments where the importance of proof of licence is not recognized. A significant cause of financial loss is when organizations cannot prove that they have purchased some licences, and need to repurchase them to prove compliance. There is also a heightened risk of loss in centralized environments to a catastrophic event such as a fire. To minimize these risks, centralized holding of licences is more appropriate, and back-up copies of licence records should be kept off-site.

B.8.3 Implementing an effective physical management system

In a small organization the physical management system for licences may be just a filing cabinet, but for most organizations this will not be sufficient.

There should be two separate parts to the system: a storage system for physical documents and other evidence; and an inventory system to record what is there. Again, in small organizations, the inventory may be kept simply in a spreadsheet, but this will usually be inadequate in large organizations. What is recommended is a document management system that can keep scanned copies of all physical documents. The physical documents can then be filed away securely without any need for normal access, as reliance is placed instead on the scanned images.

Some documentation that legally may form part of the proof of licence should already be covered by other document management systems (e.g. invoices and contracts). Depending on the functionality of the relevant systems, there may be no need to do anything further. Alternatively, it may be more practical to include copies of such documentation in the licensing document management system. It is sometimes difficult for organizations to retrieve copies of old invoices when they are needed several years later, after accounting system changes or archiving.

B.9 OTHER COMMON SOFTWARE LICENSING PROBLEMS

The following are some other common problem areas that have not already been specifically discussed:

- **Subcontractors/agents** When contractors are appointed it should be clear who is responsible for which licences. The organization will usually be responsible for any software it installs on the contractor's machines, and for the relevant licences.
- **Partially owned subsidiaries** Volume-licensing agreements may have conditions specifying which entities may purchase licences under the agreements. A common problem is that these terms may be breached by providing software to affiliates that do not qualify.

Appendix C:
ISO SAM/ITAM

C

Appendix C: ISO SAM/ITAM

Edition 3 of ISO/IEC 19770-1 IT asset management systems – requirements (hereafter referred to as the ISO ITAM standard) has been written on the basis of the generic ISO asset management standard ISO 55001: 2014 Asset management – management systems – requirements, with changes. As a result, Edition 3 of the ISO ITAM standard includes virtually all the requirements text of ISO 55001, but with additional text to reflect the extra requirements for dealing with IT assets, and in particular the requirements for dealing with software and licensing. There is only one significant change from ISO 55001, which is to handle risk more extensively in the same way as ISO/IEC 27001 for information security management. The ISO ITAM standard also defines the lifecycle and functional management processes, which are not defined in ISO 55001.

C.1 PROCESS OVERVIEW

Chapter 1 provides an overview of the ITAMS, as shown in Figure 1.2. In many respects the figure mirrors the structure of the ISO ITAM management system standard (MSS), which is as follows:

- The top grouping of processes in Figure 1.2 is 'management system processes for IT asset management'; these are largely the ISO requirements for all MSSs.
- The second grouping of processes in Figure 1.2 is 'functional management processes for IT assets'. These are specific to ISO ITAM, except 'change management', which is included in the mandatory ISO text. The full list of these processes and their respective tiers is given in Table C.1.

- The third grouping of processes in Figure 1.2 is 'lifecycle management processes for IT assets'. These are specific to ISO ITAM. The full list of these processes and their respective tiers is also given in Table C.1.

These processes are also explained in Chapter 10.

C.2 TIERS

A tier is a grouping of process areas. There are three tiers described in Edition 3 of the ISO ITAM IT asset management standard (ISO/IEC 19770-1:2017), as shown in Figure C.1. The three tiers are as follows:

- **Tier 1: Trustworthy data** Should ensure that the organization not only meets the general requirements of MSSs, but also has reasonable assurance in the trustworthiness of all data (including data needed for licence compliance). The grouping constitutes four of the eight functional management processes (see Figure 10.2).
- **Tier 2: Lifecycle integration** Comprises the processes that relate to the IT asset lifecycle (see Figure 10.3).
- **Tier 3: Optimization** Constitutes the remaining four of the eight IT asset functional management processes. This tier goes beyond assurance for licence compliance to providing reasonable assurance about the optimized use of IT assets (see Figure 10.2).

Tiers 1, 2 and 3 provide a sequence for the implementation of SAM/ITAM processes to a quality level sufficient for certification, although all the processes will need to exist to some extent regardless

Table C.1 Tiers 1–3 and their processes, attributes, capabilities, outcomes, benefits and values

Tier	Processes	Asset management culture	Organizational capability and outcomes	IT issues/benefits	Business value
1	1. Change management 2. Data management 3. Licence management 4. Security management	**Reactive** Reacting to operational events and alarms and is only as good as the quality of the management tools, especially detection and discovery	**Operational capability** 1. Trustworthy record of the current asset estate 2. Improved licence compliance	1. Duplicated and wasted assets 2. Greater 'shadow IT' spend 3. Increased diversity and complexity of IT assets 4. Redundant assets not identified and reused 5. Excessive support and management of assets 6. Greater security risks through shadow IT and redundant assets	1. Known asset estate 2. Reasonable assurance of licence compliance 3. Reduced exposure to many security risks
2	1. Specification 2. Acquisition 3. Development 4. Release 5. Deployment 6. Operation 7. Retirement	**Active** Good interfaces with change management and project management. Influences the acquisition of asset purchases	**Tactical capability** 1. Consistent management of the asset lifecycles 2. Reharvesting and re-purposing of assets	1. Reduced duplication and wastage of assets 2. Less 'shadow IT' spend 3. Reduced diversity and complexity of IT assets 4. Increased reuse and re-purposing of assets 5. Reduced support and management costs	1. Consistent response to changes and projects 2. Improved agility in response to new requirements 3. Reduced exposure to unsupported assets 4. Reduced costs dealing with security incidents

Tier	Processes	Asset management culture	Organizational capability and outcomes	IT issues/benefits	Business value
3	1. Relationship and contract management 2. Financial management 3. Service level management 4. Other risk management	**Proactive** Proactive management of the acquisition of assets. Well-defined asset strategy with a defined set of preferred services, systems and assets	**Strategic capability** 1. Strategic planning 2. Improved acquisition with a preferred set of assets	1. Minimal duplication and wastage of assets 2. Centralizes and consistent purchasing of assets, with minimal 'shadow IT' spend 3. Exploitation of assets 4. Integrated set of assets, systems and services 5. Automated and integrated management with minimal support costs 6. Improved partner negotiation and engagement with better contracts 7. Improved strategic planning	1. Greater agility in response to major new business requirements 2. Reduced service costs to the business 3. Integrated set of business-facing services, systems and assets 4. Improved strategic planning and business alignment 5. Improved management information and decision-making; increased security 6. Improved service quality, continuity and availability

of the tier being certified. The attributes, capabilities, outcomes, benefits and values associated with each of these tiers are summarized in Table C.1.

The groupings of process areas for each tier may be assessed separately, but cumulatively. For example, Tier 1 processes may be assessed by themselves. Tier 2 processes may also be assessed by themselves, but for conformance purposes Tier 1 processes must continue to conform as well. For assessing conformance with Tier 3 processes, both Tier 1 and Tier 2 processes must continue to conform.

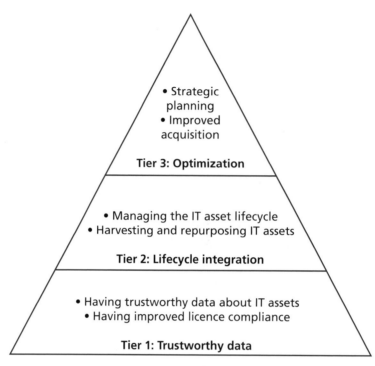

Figure C.1 The tiers of ISO/IEC 19770-1: the IT asset management system standard

Appendix D:
Technological enablers

Appendix D: Technological enablers

D.1 THE NEED FOR TECHNOLOGICAL ENABLERS

Although there have been major advances over the past decades in managing specific issues for SAM/ITAM, this has been achieved mainly by specific tools for specific types of software or for software from specific publishers. The result is a need to manage a wide variety of complex and non-interoperable tools which produce results that are difficult to consolidate. Furthermore, different tools used for the same task often produce different results, such as for software discovery. A staggering amount of specialist expertise and manual intervention is required to make it all work. As a result, some of the job is often done poorly or not at all.

The ISO Working Group responsible for SAM and ITAM standards (ISO/IEC JTC1 SC7 WG21, known as WG21) has been addressing these issues. It has developed a series of 'information structure' standards to increase the accuracy and completeness of SAM/ITAM data, while facilitating the automation of SAM/ITAM processes and the interoperability of SAM/ITAM tools. These standards are the technological enablers that are the subject of this appendix.

For an overview of all current and proposed WG21 information structure standards, see the WG21 Strategic Plan referenced in Further information. This appendix focuses on the following standards already published and in use as of 2017:

- **ISO/IEC 19770-2:2015 Software identification (SWID) tag** Provides for the authoritative identification of software and can also provide additional authoritative metadata for the management of that software, including security automation. It is installed together with the associated software.
- **ISO/IEC 19770-3:2016 Entitlement (Ent) schema** Provides for the encoding of entitlements and related licensing terms and conditions. It is intended to be supplied at the time a licence is obtained, typically via a different route from that of the software itself for volume-licensing programmes.
- **ISO/IEC 19770-4:2017 Resource utilization measurement (RUM)** Provides a standard logging structure for recording usage information, whether against licence entitlements or any other type of resource. It is created at the time of usage. How it is created depends on the nature of the measurement to be made, and the capabilities of the tools or other software making the measurement.

All of the above are currently implemented primarily as XML schemas, but they can be implemented in other ways (e.g. using JavaScript Object Notation or JSON). More details about each are given below. The XML schema definitions (XSDs) for all three standards are also available for public download from the URLs given in Further information (XML and XSD are defined in the abbreviations and glossary; information about JSON is available on the internet).

Note that a new information structure standard for a hardware identification tag, similar in concept to the software identification tag, is planned. When this is implemented in the marketplace it should be another significant enabler for the automation of SAM/ITAM.

D.2 SOFTWARE IDENTIFICATION TAG

D.2.1 SWID overview

There are already two editions of the SWID tag standard, the first from 2009 (ISO/IEC 19770-2:2009) and the second from 2015 (ISO/IEC 19770-2:2015). The 2009 edition was revised in the 2015 edition to facilitate its implementation by publishers, and also in particular to facilitate security automation by end-users. This appendix describes the 2015 edition, which is already being widely adopted, driven in significant measure by the security community. Further information about the security benefits of SWID tags is given in section 14.5. This appendix is concerned with more general issues related to SWID tags.

The following are key characteristics and capabilities of the SWID tag:

- authoritative identification of software, whether installed or not, including all relevant details, such as version
- authoritative identification of patches and added details (e.g. for in-house configuration information) without affecting the integrity of the original SWID tag
- ability to provide additional metadata which can be used for security automation, in particular for linking to vulnerability databases, and for providing footprint information, directly or through linkages which allow for validating the authenticity of all files included with a distribution

- ability to sign SWID tags to ensure provenance and authenticity
- ability for SWID tags to be created by publishers, by in-house teams, or by third parties where appropriate.

The US National Institute of Standards and Technology (NIST) has issued guidelines for the creation of interoperable SWID tags (Waltermire *et al.*, 2016). Although this is particularly directed at US government users, it is useful for all organizations.

The need for, and value of, SWID tags can perhaps be best understood by explaining the differences between how software discovery works with and without them, as described below. For further explanations specifically related to security, see Chapter 14.

D.2.2 Software discovery process using an application recognition library

When a discovery process is executed on a computing device by a tool that does not use SWID tags, the tool may do various things depending on the operating system or device involved. In general, it will collect data on various artefacts on the device, including any centralized installation records (add/remove programs on Windows, RPM installation database on Linux, system profiler on the Apple Mac, etc.); a list of all executable files; and, potentially, additional artefacts of data that are more specific to the device. This data is then put through an application recognition database to attempt to identify the software products installed.

This approach can experience the following problems:

- Organizations may change or remove the names of software titles installed in the centralized installation database.

- Two different products may share a set of executable files based on the installation options that have been chosen.
- A product that is part of a suite can be identified as being a stand-alone product.
- A product that is installed as a stand-alone product can be identified as being part of a suite.
- Each recognition library is proprietary, so typically the resulting data can only be used for the purpose of the tool with which it is associated and the data cannot easily be compared or consolidated with data from other IT tools.
- Unless the discovery process is specifically designed for patch reporting, patches are often not properly identified.
- Depending on the discovery tool, software that runs using an interpreted language (for example, Java, Perl and Net) may not be properly identified.

Since recognition libraries are created based on data that the tool provider has seen, there are other problems with this approach:

- Software that has not been seen by the tool provider generally will not be included in the list.
- Software that an organization has created internally may not be able to be added to the list.
- There is always a delay when a new product version is released before the recognition library is updated.
- If the tool provider enters incorrect data for a software product, that title will be misidentified.

D.2.3 Software discovery process using publisher-supplied and digitally signed SWID tags

Contrast the above with what happens when a software publisher provides SWID tags that are digitally signed. When SWID tags are provided, discovery processes have the following benefits:

- exact details of which software product and version is installed on the device
- exact details of any patches that are installed and to which product(s) each patch applies
- normalized data that can be shared and automatically compared with the data in other IT tools and systems
- no delay in identification data since the data is sent with the software
- ability to identify any interpreted application
- ability for organizations to include the identification of internally built software in a manner that all discovery tools can utilize (reducing the risk of tool provider lock-in)
- proper identification of suites of software as well as the knowledge of which components of the suite are installed
- no impact on the integrity of the discovery data regardless of how the software may have been configured by the customer.

Since the data is provided by the publisher of the software, a number of IT operations can be automated. For example, a customer could implement a process whereby a system requests a daily list of all patches or upgrades available from a specified publisher and automatically generates a report that includes details of the software to which the patch/upgrade applies and how many devices in the organization are impacted, based purely on inventory data.

Additionally, from a security perspective, if all software on the device is tagged and contains the file manifest (payload), IT tools can easily and automatically identify if new (and potentially rogue) software is installed, if a patch or upgrade did not install properly, or if an executable file from a publisher is modified using anything other than an approved update (such as a patch or upgrade).

D.3 ENTITLEMENT SCHEMA

The entitlement (Ent) schema, as defined by ISO/IEC 19770-3:2016, provides for the encoding of entitlements and related licensing terms and conditions. It is intended to be supplied at the time a licence is obtained, typically via a different route from that of the software itself for volume-licensing programmes. Ideally it will be supplied and signed by the publisher selling the licence, but it can also be created by the end-user organization or by third parties (e.g. resellers or SAM managed service providers).

The Ent does not constitute a licence itself, but rather is expected just to encode the most important information from a licence to facilitate automating the management of licences, such as quantity and purchase reference information. In theory, it can be used to encode all licensing terms and conditions, and could then be considered to fully represent a licence, but to make that practical would probably first require significant normalization of licensing terms and conditions in the marketplace.

The following are key characteristics and capabilities of the Ent:

- authoritative identification of an entitlement/ licence, with sufficient information to allow linkage with instances of installed software and/ or with software utilization
- ability to create and link additional Ents without affecting the integrity of the original Ents (e.g. to reflect licences for upgrades)

- ability to create and use 'management' Ents linked to initial entitlements for the purposes of allocating and transferring entitlements to different units or organizations
- ability for organizations to extract basic information for use in simple spreadsheet control approaches, while retaining the possibility of using software tools to exploit the full potential of the Ent with the complex relationships it can encode.

D.4 RESOURCE UTILIZATION MEASUREMENT

RUM, as defined by ISO/IEC 19770-4, is a standard logging structure for recording usage information, whether against licence entitlements or any other type of resource. It is based on existing practice that is being standardized. The RUM is most likely to be created at the time of usage. How it is created depends on the nature of the measurement to be made and the capabilities of the tools or other software making the measurement.

The following are key characteristics and capabilities of the RUM:

- authoritative identification of a usage measure, with sufficient information to allow linkage with instances of installed software and/or with software entitlements
- authoritative definition of a usage measure, sufficient to allow both its creation, and its utilization, by different tools from different tool providers.

Appendix E: Possible ITAM database contents

E

Appendix E: Possible ITAM database contents

This appendix gives suggestions for the possible physical storage contents and corresponding electronic databases for ITAM. See section 11.2 for how these relate to ITAM overall, and to the ITIL concepts of the DML and the CMS.

Each organization will need to decide what data it needs. Some of the contents of the ITAM database will be driven by software licensing metrics. Furthermore, if these possible database contents are being used as part of tool selection, particular emphasis should be placed on the licensing metrics associated with the greatest potential licensing exposures.

Some of the information that may be stored in an ITAM database is not 'raw' but processed or calculated information; for example, calculations of effective licences held, usage against licence entitlements, or licence reconciliation calculations. It is not realistic to manage ITAM without automated tools, including for these calculations. This appendix provides guidance on what information would typically be held, but does not consider the question of tools needed to generate that information.

E.1 COMMON CMS CONFIGURATION ITEM ATTRIBUTES

All CIs need certain basic information, which is applicable in principle to all the remaining types of information described in this appendix. Common data needed for CIs will typically include attribute information (e.g. CI name and description);

relationships with other CIs; and financial data, where relevant, including to facilitate reconciliation to financial systems.

E.2 GENERIC ITAM AUTHORIZATIONS

Organizations require broad classes of authorizations for different types of IT assets, including hardware and software. Every organization needs to determine which authorizations are appropriate for it, and how they will be specified. Authorizations can, for example, be of different types (e.g. for security, technical, purchasing, finance and managerial), at different organizational levels (e.g. at the organization-wide, unit-wide or function-specific levels), at different levels of hardware granularity (e.g. by type, such as routers; by specific vendor; and by specific model), and excluded or included (e.g. for blacklisting or whitelisting).

The authorizations that an organization establishes should be well documented and readily accessible for the purposes of checking individual instances against them.

Authorizations may also be relevant at the level of unique instances (e.g. of hardware and software), and such authorizations will generally be recorded as part of the respective inventories.

E.3 HARDWARE INVENTORY

Currently there are no generic and comprehensive standards for the identification of hardware. A personal computer, for example, may have many uniquely identifiable components that may be changed without affecting the effective identity of that personal computer. There are, however, some standards (proprietary or de facto) for identifying individual instances of some types of hardware, such as MAC addresses or serial numbers.

Each organization should determine the level to which individual items of hardware need to be identified and inventoried. Physically consolidated entities (such as complete PCs) typically will be uniquely identified and physically tagged. Practice varies for component parts. For example, an organization may inventory major component parts of PCs (such as SSDs), but not other components (such as CPUs) or accessories (such as mice).

Similar cost and purchase history information should be maintained as for software licence inventories (see section E.6).

Hardware inventories should also include any information needed to facilitate software licensing calculations, such as core counts for servers.

E.4   SOFTWARE INVENTORY

Refer to ISO/IEC 19770-2 (Software identification (SWID) tag standard) for its definitions of elements and attributes of software. This is an international standard for how software is identified, the metadata needed for its use, and how patches and other information can be provided without losing the integrity of the original information (see also Appendix D). Software inventory management tools should include the ability to use SWID tags fully. Additional information (such as installation date) is still generally required.

E.5   SERVICES INVENTORY

ITAM needs to control an increasing number of services, of which inventories need to be kept, with details such as renewal dates. Services may include hardware maintenance, software support, cloud-based services (such as IaaS, PaaS and SaaS), training and consultancy, and outsourced services, possibly including SAM/ITAM itself.

E.6   LICENCE INVENTORY

The licence inventory is a list of licence transactions. Licence transactions are the unique individual occurrences when licences are obtained or otherwise managed. There are many different types of licence, such as full licences, upgrade licences and maintenance licences (see also Appendix B for an overview of licensing). However, it may be necessary to obtain several different licences to have one effective full licence or entitlement. Effective licences, or entitlements, are addressed in section E.7.

'Proof of licence' should be cited as part of the licence inventory. This proof may be in the form of publisher licence confirmations (especially for volume licensing), COAs (especially for some retail products), and may require other types of documentation (see section B.8 for more information).

Reference should be made to ISO/IEC 19770-3 (Entitlement schema or 'Ent') for its definitions of elements and attributes of licence/entitlement transactions. This provides an international standard for how licence/entitlement information can be encoded and managed, including allocations and transfers, without losing the integrity of the information (see also Appendix D). Software licence management tools should include the ability to use Ents fully.

Not all licence transactions will be purchases. Open-source licences, for example, should be inventoried, but it may not be appropriate to record most typical procurement details. Another example is technology guarantees, which are effectively upgrade transactions (they allow the upgrading of licences for one version of a product if purchased within a specified period before the next version is released). The management-type transactions provided by ISO/IEC 19770-3 (Entitlement schema) for allocations, transfers, etc. are also valid licence transactions.

E.7 EFFECTIVE LICENCES

Achieving licence compliance requires ensuring that all 'usage' (see section E.8) is covered by appropriate entitlements. These entitlements are sometimes determined by individual licences (such as for full retail licences), but often they require the determination of effective licences which take into account the combined effects of multiple individual licences. The determination of effective licences can be one of the most complex tasks in licence management. It depends not only on the more obvious relationships between the simple concepts of full, upgrade and maintenance licences, but also on potentially complex terms and conditions (e.g. relating to which combinations are valid at what dates). There can be further complications related to the determination of which supporting licences can be used within large organizations where the different licence types may have been purchased by different but related legal entities. Another issue is knowing for which versions of the software a given licence provides use rights (e.g. via downgrade rights), given these potentially complex combinations of underlying licences, and the need to match actual usage (which might be of multiple versions) with effective licences.

The detailed way in which effective licences are calculated, and how these results are presented and stored, is currently managed by different software tools in their own proprietary ways. It may also be done 'manually', but it is complex and requires exceptionally high knowledge and skill levels. The ISO Entitlement schema standard is expected to facilitate effective licensing calculations in the future, through better and more authoritative specification of the ways that different licences can be linked. However, this will take some time to develop in the marketplace.

The effective licence figures should ideally be linked to where they are used (e.g. to specific devices, people or sites), but this is not yet a common practice.

E.8 LICENCE USAGE

Each licence has its own definition of how its 'usage' is measured. Some definitions are simple, such as 'per installation'. Others can be highly complex, such as for processor- or core-based licences in virtualized environments, and for related client-access-based metrics.

Because of the extreme variability of how usage is defined, there is similar variability in the mechanisms needed to measure that usage. ISO/IEC 19770-4 (resource utilization measurement) provides an industry-standard specification for an information structure to record usage (see also Appendix D). In practical terms, it must be assumed that each organization will need a number of different mechanisms to measure usage. It is beyond the scope of this guide to address this in detail.

The results of the usage measurements, however, should be stored in the ITAM database in a consistent and controlled way. Historical usage information should be maintained, not just the current or most recent results.

E.9 MEDIA INVENTORY

There needs to be inventory control over physical media as well as over electronic distribution copies of software which are often located on servers. Some specific organizational approaches have been recommended by software publishers for their own volume-licensing media.

E.10 SOURCE DOCUMENTATION

Many types of documentation need to be filed, including contracts, proof-of-licence documentation, invoices, price lists, and correspondence with resellers and publishers. Where the documentation is physical, it is recommended that copies be scanned and filed in an electronic document management system, if possible, to ensure better availability of the information as well as greater security for the source documents. An indexing system will be needed to allow cross-referencing from different databases.

Some documentation is now available electronically (e.g. software publisher licence confirmations, terms and conditions documents and general licensing information).

E.11 WORKING DOCUMENTATION

It is desirable to file many types of working documentation formally, particularly licence compliance reconciliations, other reviews and compliance checks.

E.12 GUIDANCE DOCUMENTATION

It is good practice to file copies of SAM guidance documentation from all sources, including software publishers, resellers and professional sources (such as this guide).

Appendix F: Choosing a SAM/ITAM partner

F

Appendix F: Choosing a SAM/ITAM partner

Just about every organization working in any area related to SAM, ITAM or licensing will claim to offer SAM/ITAM consultancy and related services. It is important to separate the marketing hype from true capability and to determine whether a potential SAM/ITAM partner will be able to provide true value at a reasonable cost. Table F.1 identifies some criteria worth investigating when selecting a partner. The focus of this appendix is on choosing a SAM/ITAM consultant, but much of it can be applied to other types of SAM/ITAM partner (see Chapter 12 for a more general discussion of the types of partners and the services they provide).

The most important selection criterion will usually be the skills and experience of the individuals who will be responsible for the services to be provided. This is even more important than the overall experience of the organization for which they work.

Where it is appropriate to have two or more partners working together, at least one should have extensive and practical current licensing knowledge for software within the project scope.

Table F.1 Importance criteria for possible SAM/ITAM partners

Ref.	Criteria	Rank	Comments
	Qualifications and capabilities of the organization		
1	Can the organization demonstrate experience for the type of assistance sought?	H	
2	Does the organization have established methodologies and tools for the type of assistance sought?	H	
3	How long has the organization been providing the type of assistance sought?	M	
4	What quality of licensing expertise is expected to be applied as part of the service to be provided? Examine details of people, training and qualifications, and length of time in jobs	H	One of the most important issues in the selection of a potential partner. The expertise needs to be realistically available, and applied to the work without having to make exceptional requests

Table continues

Table F.1 *continued*

Ref.	Criteria	Rank	Comments
5	If the service requires determination of effective licensing, what relevant tools and methodologies can be demonstrated?	H	One of the most complex issues in licence compliance is the determination of current effective licences taking into account all past licence purchases including full and upgrade products of various types; upgrade insurance and its timing relative to release dates of new versions; and detailed contractual issues about how previous licences relate to site licences (i.e. are they subsumed by the new licences, or are they separate and available for redeployment?)
6	Does the organization offer other related services that may complement the type of assistance currently sought?	L	May create synergies, but may also create conflicts of interest (see below)
7	Where is the service available geographically?	L	More important for multinational organizations
8	In what languages is the service available?	L	More important for multinational organizations
9	How old is the organization?	L	
10	How financially strong is the organization?	M	More important for organizations where there may need to be a long-term relationship (e.g. with tool providers or managed service providers)
SAM/ITAM focus			
11	How many people does the organization have, globally and locally, dedicated full-time to providing SAM/ITAM-type services (not full-time equivalents of people doing other work as well)?	M	A good indicator of the seriousness of an organization about SAM/ITAM
12	Are SAM/ITAM services provided by a dedicated unit or out of a more generalist unit?	M	A good indicator of the seriousness of an organization about SAM/ITAM

Ref.	Criteria	Rank	Comments
Conflicts of interest			
13	Is the organization primarily dependent on a particular publisher for most of its work?	M	A close relationship with a particular software publisher can be an advantage in terms of detailed knowledge of that software publisher's products, but it needs to be assessed against the possible conflicts of interest involved (e.g. advocating that software publisher's products inappropriately, or leaking confidential information back to that software publisher)
14	Does the organization have vested interests in other areas that might affect the independence of its SAM/ITAM services (e.g. selling licences, selling and/or installing SAM/ITAM tools or providing managed services)?	M	Involvement in any of these areas can be an advantage because of the additional knowledge it gives to the organization, but it needs to be assessed against the possible conflicts of interest involved
15	Does the organization offer its services on a fee basis rather than related to the sale of other products?	M	Fee-based services are generally preferable from an independence point of view
16	Does it appear that the service is being offered as a 'loss-leader' with the objective of cross-selling other services in the future (e.g. as a result of knowing more about internal IT plans)?	H	Loss-leaders may represent false savings. The provider will typically not be able to justify the quality-in-depth that the job requires, and the work may be biased to ensure the creation of new revenue opportunities
Qualifications and capabilities of the principal individuals proposed			
17	Does the individual have demonstrated experience for the type of assistance sought? Over what period?	H	Very important
18	Can the individual answer relevant detailed questions without research during initial discussions?	H	Proof of capabilities
19	Does the individual have qualifications for the type of assistance sought (e.g. licensing qualifications from software publishers)?	M	

Table continues

Table F.1 *continued*

Ref.	Criteria	Rank	Comments
References			
20	Can you talk privately to at least two referees for whom the organization has previously provided similar services, and get good feedback?	H	Very important
Other questions			
21	How well does the organization control its own software and IT assets? Ask to see a live demonstration and talk to end-users	M	Demonstrates how serious the organization is about SAM/ITAM
22	Does the organization have any other general certifications or qualifications (e.g. ISO certifications or software publisher certifications)?	L	The question is how relevant the certifications are to the services being requested

Key to importance weighting: L = low, M = medium, H = high

Appendix G:
Partner contracting

Appendix G: Partner contracting

G.1 OVERVIEW

This appendix concerns the SAM/ITAM implications of contracting for IT services, particularly for outsourcing, managed services and cloud services.

Some of the most significant developments impacting SAM/ITAM result from changes in who provides IT services, and the corresponding contractual relationships. Even more important than the technological issues involved (especially with cloud computing), are the issues of changing and mixed responsibilities. These bring both benefits (which are expected) and bad effects (often unexpected).

'Outsourcing' is a term generally used to refer to the transfer of all or most activities of an entire unit to an external provider, such as all IT development or all IT operations, and sometimes includes the transfer of personnel. 'Managed service' is the term generally used to refer to the transfer of one discrete service to an external provider. Often the visible part of that managed service will be provided on the premises, but there may be an off-premises component. Cloud-based services such as SaaS, PaaS and IaaS generally provide more computer-specific services based entirely off the premises.

Some specific examples of these scenarios, and their implications for SAM/ITAM, are as follows:

- **Full outsourcing of IT** Offers some of the greatest immediate savings, but also some of the greatest constraints in terms of longer-term flexibility and responsiveness. When the contracting arrangements do not properly provide for licence management, it may result in some of the most serious underlicensing situations.
- **Managed infrastructure services** Effectively includes ITAM and SAM. Depending on a number of factors, including the contractual provisions for licence management, it can be a major success for ITAM and SAM, but it can be a disaster.
- **Managed SAM/ITAM services** May be referred to as SAM as a Service (SAMaaS) and will typically include licence management and licence compliance services. This can be highly successful, as it should bring both good tools and competent licensing expertise into the organization. But not all such services are equally good.
- **Procurement-related outsourcing** May take various forms, for example:
  - capture of orders via an external provider's order-entry application placed on the end-customer's intranet, linked to reseller systems
  - full IT procurement processing via implants within an organization (e.g. the IT procurement function may be largely subcontracted to a specialist team from an outsourcer, but operating fully within the user organization).
- **Contracted licensing expertise** An increasingly popular way for organizations to obtain the specialized software licensing expertise they need without having to develop and maintain it internally. Typically a certain amount of licensing expertise would be contracted in on a regular

basis. This could be considered a baseline best-practice approach in SAM for all but the largest organizations, and even for them, it is probably justified as a quality assurance best-practice.

■ **Cloud services** Cloud computing does not obviate the need for licence management or indeed most software management. Although the cloud computing model can eliminate such issues in specific cases, the following complications are likely:

● Cloud services deal primarily with the server side. Where they relate to infrastructure and platform (e.g. database) services, the corresponding client-side hardware and software generally still require full SAM/ITAM management. Any reduction in server licence management will be more than compensated for by monitoring and managing the cloud service provider contracts, usage and performance, which are new requirements.

● The 'simple' cloud licensing models assume pure subscription-based licensing, which makes no use of any equivalent existing licences owned, so they are effectively thrown away. Using 'legacy' licences in a cloud environment, when possible, adds another layer of complexity to licence management, rather than simplifying it.

● Licensing can be dependent on changes on the server side that are outside the user's control. For example, server hardware consolidation or upgrading by a cloud service provider can have a major impact on licence requirements.

● The need for monitoring of cloud usage, performance, costs and contracts goes up more than the need for managing server-side licensing goes down. Cloud contracts can expand easily, based on peak usage levels, but do not reduce easily. They tend to extend automatically unless they are closely monitored and managed, although they may be unknown to the IT department. They may also present particular data confidentiality issues. There tend to be many such contracts, from many providers, all potentially with the same concerns, but with different detailed management requirements.

G.2 ADVANTAGES AND DISADVANTAGES

The typical advantages claimed for contracting external services are reduced costs, improved expertise and improved responsiveness. For the purposes of licence management, the improved expertise is to be expected only if the service provider has the expertise needed and the contract clearly provides for it. Service providers have contract managers who ensure contract compliance, but do not provide additional unpaid services.

The following are some of the disadvantages of subcontracting relationships from the perspective of SAM/ITAM:

■ **Loss of visibility** Information that is controlled by the service provider, including for SAM/ITAM purposes, will be lost to the organization unless the relevant requirements for access to the information are clearly specified contractually. This applies equally to the cloud as it does to managed services such as infrastructure services.

■ **Loss of flexibility and responsiveness** If a service is not provided for in the contract, do not expect it, or be prepared to pay extra for it. Licensing audits, or preparing for the possibility of them, are a case in point.

- **Need for additional contract management and monitoring skills** Good contract management does not happen by itself.
- **Continued need for sufficient expertise to exercise oversight responsibilities** Even if significant performance responsibilities have been contracted out, the legal liability will remain with the organization. As a result, the organization must retain sufficient expertise to monitor the performance of the contracted party. In the case of licence compliance, someone internal must retain responsibility for oversight of licence compliance, and of everything that is being done by contracted parties related to it. This internal role needs the expertise to discharge that responsibility competently.

Overall, remember that there are trade-offs for the purposes of SAM/ITAM; increased simplicity for the end-user organization typically means increased cost, as does increased responsiveness.

Key message

For the organization to manage its IT costs effectively, including through the use of outsourcing, managed services and cloud services, SAM/ITAM will need to work in highly complex environments.

G.3 PROBLEM AREAS

G.3.1 Uncontrolled subcontracting

A growing problem area, especially with cloud computing, is the proliferation of subcontracting directly by end-users without the involvement or knowledge of IT or procurement. (This is a major and increasing component of 'shadow IT'.) The cost of individual contracts may not be significant, but their cumulative impact can be. Furthermore, they may present some significant issues related to security and loss of data integrity.

There is no simple solution to this problem. Although it is essential to have robust policies in place concerning end-user contracting, simply having a policy is not sufficient. The most important steps to take to control this area are related to (a) discovery, and (b) continuing user education, often by explaining the issues that arise from failures to follow policy in discovered cases (see also section 4.5).

G.3.2 Licensing

The biggest issues resulting from subcontracting where IT is involved are almost always related to software licensing. For example:

- **Unclear responsibility and accountability for licensing** If the contracted role has any potential impact on licence management or licence compliance, but its responsibilities related to licence management are not clearly specified contractually, they will probably be done poorly, if at all.
- **Management lack of understanding of legal and contractual responsibilities** Management may wrongly think it has contracted away its accountability for licence compliance via outsourcing or managed service contracts. Although it is possible to contract out licence management, the entity that is using the licences will always be accountable for licence compliance.
- **Management unwillingness to enforce software use policies** Because management believes that software management is no longer its concern, it may be unwilling to enforce reasonable policies needed for good SAM/ITAM (e.g. it may allow anyone to install anything on their devices).

■ **Lack of clarity concerning responsibility for licensing of contractors' employees and software** Management may not realize that the end-user organization is likely to be responsible for much contractor licensing in outsourcing and managed service situations.

■ **Lack of clarity about ownership of licences** Outsourcers have sometimes retained ownership of perpetual licences they purchased on behalf of end-users.

■ **Lack of sufficient licensing skill and knowledge within the organization** Skill and knowledge are necessary to exercise the necessary oversight of subcontracted activity.

■ **Unintended consequences of split responsibilities** There can be unexpected impacts on licensing that result from how outsourcing responsibilities are allocated (e.g. a cloud service provider that increases server capacity to maintain response times may unwittingly create a major licensing exposure for the software being run on those servers).

G.3.3 Overlapping ownership/ responsibilities for hardware, data and software

There are increasingly overlapping ownerships and responsibilities for hardware, data and software within IT, and most of these situations involve outsourcing, managed services or cloud services. Respective responsibilities need to be clearly specified in all cases, whether in contractual terms and conditions, or in policies (which need to be formally acknowledged by individuals where relevant). For example:

■ **Device ownership and direct custodial responsibility** Devices may belong to many different organizations, including lessors. What is important is who has direct custodial responsibility for the equipment. This may be the organization itself, individuals (especially employees and contractors) and service providers. IT asset inventories will need to include all assets that might have control implications for the organization, even if the organization does not own them or have direct custodial responsibility. (This also means that it might be impossible to reconcile such assets to the organization's financial reporting system.)

■ **Data ownership** Confidential data belonging to the organization is often accessed from, and/or held, on devices owned by others, whether individuals (especially employees and contractors) or service providers. Likewise, personal data (e.g. pictures, emails and social media) belonging to those individuals is frequently held on devices not owned by them but by the organization or third parties. To ensure adequate control over data belonging to the organization (e.g. when personal devices are lost), there needs to be careful policy crafting, acceptance by users, and technology to enable and enforce those policies.

■ **Software (licence) ownership** Software licensed to one person or organization may be installed on hardware belonging to a different person or organization. For example, personal software might be installed on smartphones provided by the organization, and likewise on PCs provided by the organization (depending on company policies and on technological control measures in place). With cloud services, some of the software may be provided by the cloud service provider, and other software may be provided by the user organization. In such cases the licensing implications may be complex (e.g. during an audit a publisher may find the organization responsible for the licensing of software supplied by the provider or installed by employees). The organization should ensure that it knows all software for which it might possibly be considered responsible for licensing, and ensure that appropriate steps are taken (policy, contractual and technical) to eliminate or minimize that exposure.

G.3.4 Conflicts of interest

Many conflicts of interest can arise as a result of subcontracting. For example:

- **Data ownership and portability** There can be a significant issue concerning who owns what data, and how easily it can be accessed and ported elsewhere. A contractor will understandably not wish to release information that can be used for the contracting organization to obtain a competitive quote for those services (e.g. towards the end of a contract). Data ownership, access rights and portability provisions need to be contractually specified, to avoid such restrictions being encountered during the contract.

- **Territorial conflicts** There can be conflicts with other partners/outsourcers and internal units over perceived 'territories' (e.g. if there is one outsourcer for hardware and another for software and licence management).

- **Other** There can be other conflicts of interest from the outsourcer (e.g. unwillingness to move to new technology or systems, or to improve problem areas because of potential revenue impact, competitive concerns or inflexible contracts). There can also be conflicts of interest if the outsourcer performs other functions (e.g. if it is a reseller).

G.3.5 Managing the contracting lifecycle

The following are some of the challenges and problems associated with the management of the contracting lifecycle:

- **Starting a contract** When a contract is started, the basis for that start (e.g. number of users, devices etc.) may be negotiated rather than an accurate figure. It may have been understated for commercial negotiating reasons. A correct baseline needs to be established, or the data is unlikely to be corrected until a publisher audit.

- **Ending a contract** Although relations are typically good at the start of a contract, they may be poor when it ends, whether by expiry or early termination. Unless requirements at termination are clearly specified, problems can be expected.

- **Exceptional services, costs and responsiveness** Unexpected things happen, such as software publisher audits, or merger and acquisition reviews, that require additional help from the contractor. The contract needs to specify that such help will be provided, within what timeframe, and at what cost.

Key recommendations

- Have your licence compliance checked independently, even if you already have in-house licensing expertise. It is too complex an area, with too much exposure, to take chances, unless you wish to rely on publisher audits to perform your checking.

- Maintain meaningful oversight of all contracted services, including anything dealing with licence compliance and with cloud services. This means having the skills (in-house or separately contracted) to conduct that oversight. Consider hiring specialist contract management skills, or developing them internally.

■ Have clear policies about what people are allowed or not allowed to do, especially where these may impact on contracted services. These policies would include acceptable use (e.g. not installing software without authorization) and procurement (e.g. not contracting for cloud services without authorization).

■ Consider carefully the implications for SAM/ITAM of all potential contracting relationships before you sign.

Further research

Further research

REFERENCES

1E (2016) Software usage and waste report [online] https://www.1e.com/resource-center/software-usage-waste-report-2016/ [accessed 19 September 2017].

California, State of, Department of Justice, Office of the Attorney General (2016) Privacy and identity theft – press releases [online] 16 February 2016. https://oag.ca.gov/new-press-categories/privacy-identity-theft [accessed 6 September 2017].

CIS (2016) Critical security controls published as a technical report of the European Telecommunications Standards Institute. https://www.cisecurity.org/press-release/cis-controls-published-as-a-technical-report-of-the-european-telecommunications-standards-institute/ [accessed 6 September 2017].

CIS (2017) CIS controls [online] www.cisecurity.org/controls [accessed 6 September 2017].

CIS, New America (2017) Where privacy meets security [online] 28 June 2017. https://www.newamerica.org/cybersecurity-initiative/events/where-privacy-meets-security/ [accessed 6 September 2017].

Defense Standardization Program. DoD Information Technology Standards Registry (DISR) [online] www.dsp.dla.mil/Specs-Standards/List-of-DISR-documents/ [accessed 6 September 2017].

Forrester Research (2015) Report commissioned by 1E. Prevent hidden risks with enhanced software asset management. https://www.1e.com/prevent-hidden-risks-with-enhanced-software-asset-management/ [accessed 6 September 2017].

Gartner (2015) Software asset management: understanding the SAM services market for effective third-party support. ID: G00271495. https://www.gartner.com/doc/2965119/software-asset-management-understanding-sam [accessed 6 September 2017].

Gawande, Atul (2014) BBC Reith lecture series 'The Century of the System' [online] 06 December 2014. http://downloads.bbc.co.uk/radio4/open-book/2014_reith_lecture2_wellcome.pdf [accessed 6 September 2017].

ISO/IEC 19770-1 IT asset management – Part 1: IT asset management systems – requirements, clause 3.25 https://www.iso.org/standard/68531.html [accessed 12 December 2017].

ISO/IEC 19770-1 IT asset management – Part 1: IT asset management systems – requirements: Appendix C – Characteristics of IT assets https://www.iso.org/standard/68531.html [accessed 12 December 2017].

Kaplan, R. S. and Norton, D. P. (1992) The balanced scorecard – measures that drive performance. *Harvard Business Review* January–February. https://hbr.org/1992/01/the-balanced-scorecard-measures-that-drive-performance-2 [accessed 6 September 2017].

LinkedIn (2015) [online]. 8. Blog and discussion including use of checklists https://www.linkedin.com/groups/87458/87458-5961183757233844224 [cited 01 February 2017].

NIST (2014) Framework for improving critical infrastructure cybersecurity [online] 12 February 2014. www.nist.gov/sites/default/files/documents/cyberframework/cybersecurity-framework-021214.pdf [accessed 6 September 2017].

OECD (2017) Trade in counterfeit ICT goods [online] 28 March 2017. www.oecd.org/gov/risk/trade-in-counterfeit-ict-goods-9789264270848-en.htm [accessed 6 September 2017].

SANS (2017) CIS critical security controls for effective cyber defense [online] www.sans.org/critical-security-controls [accessed 6 September 2017].

Trusted Computing Group (2015) TNC SWID messages and attributes for IF-M specification [online] 1 August 2015. https://trustedcomputinggroup.org/tnc-swid-messages-attributes-if-m-specification [accessed 6 September 2017].

Waltermire, D. *et al.* (2016) Guidelines for the creation of interoperable software identification (SWID) tags – NISTIR 8060 [online] April 2016. http://dx.doi.org/10.6028/NIST.IR.8060 [accessed 6 September 2017].

White House, The (2017) Presidential executive order on strengthening the cybersecurity of federal networks and critical infrastructure [online] 11 May 2017. https://www.whitehouse.gov/the-press-office/2017/05/11/presidential-executive-order-strengthening-cybersecurity-federal [accessed 6 September 2017].

FURTHER INFORMATION

ITIL publications (physical, ebook and online)

AXELOS (2016) *ITIL Practitioner Guidance*. The Stationery Office, London.

Cabinet Office (2011) *Introduction to the ITIL Service Lifecycle*. The Stationery Office, London.

Cabinet Office (2011) *ITIL Continual Service Improvement*. The Stationery Office, London.

Cabinet Office (2011) *ITIL Service Design*. The Stationery Office, London.

Cabinet Office (2011) *ITIL Service Operation*. The Stationery Office, London.

Cabinet Office (2011) *ITIL Service Strategy*. The Stationery Office, London.

Cabinet Office (2011) *ITIL Service Transition*. The Stationery Office, London.

ITIL Glossary and Abbreviations (2011) https://www.axelos.com/corporate/media/files/glossaries/itil_2011_glossary_gb-v1-0.pdf [accessed 6 September 2017].

Office of Government Commerce (2010) *ITIL V3 Planning to Implement Service Management*. The Stationery Office, London.

Office of Government Commerce (2010) *Management of Value*. The Stationery Office, London.

ISO and ISO/IEC publications

These are available from the ISO website (www.iso.org). Some of these standards are freely available, but most must be purchased.

ISO/IEC 19770 IT asset management family of standards (including the ISO/IEC 19770-1 ITAM management system standard)

ISO/IEC 20000 IT service management family of standards (including the ISO/IEC 20000-1 IT service management system standard)

ISO/IEC 9000 Quality management family of standards (including the ISO 9001 quality management system standard)

ISO/IEC 27000 Information security family of standards (including ISO/IEC 27001 information security management system standard)

ISO/IEC 55000 Asset management family of standards (including ISO 55001 asset management system standard)

ISO Directives Part 1 Annex SL (2016) for common requirements for all management system standards

ISO/IEC JTC1 SC7 WG21 IT asset management working group publications

These are freely available from ISO and from the WG21 website as indicated.

ISO/IEC 19770-5 Overview and terminology. Available from http://standards.iso.org/ittf/ PubliclyAvailableStandards/c068291_ ISOIEC_19770-5_2015.zip

XSD for ISO/IEC 19770-2:2015 Software identification tag. Available from standards.iso.org/ iso/19770/-2/2015-current/schema.xsd

XSD for ISO/IEC 19770-3:2016 Entitlement schema. Available from http://standards.iso.org/iso/19770/-3/2015/schema.xsd

XSD for ISO/IEC 19770-4 Resource utilization measurement. Available from http://standards.iso.org/iso-iec/19770/-4/ed-1/schema.xsd

SC7 WG21 Strategic Plan. Available from standards.iso.org/iso/19770/StratPlan

Other materials

The critical security controls, also known as the CIS controls

The CSCs were originally developed by the SANS Institute, and information about them is still available at www.sans.org/critical-security-controls. They have now been taken over by the Center for Internet Security, which now refers to them as the CIS CSCs, and more simply as the 'CIS controls'. See www.cisecurity.org/controls

Corporate governance codes

A good source of information about, and links to, corporate governance codes worldwide by country has been created by the European Corporate Governance Institute. It is available at www.ecgi.org/codes/all_codes.php

Supplementary materials for the ITIL SAM/ITAM guide

Some supplementary materials for this guide are planned as white papers on the AXELOS website (www.axelos.com/case-study-and-white-paper-search). Others are planned to be available from www.m-assure.com. These materials are expected to cover the following topics, and more may be added over time.

Guidance on selecting ITAM tools

Detailed suggestions for the contents of ITAM databases and libraries

Overview of services provided by SAM/ITAM partners

Guidance on documenting a SAM/ITAM process

Processes for review and improvement

Overview of the common approach now being used for all ISO management system standards

An overview of ITIL for ITAM practitioners new to ITIL

Abbreviations and glossary

Abbreviations

BaU	business as usual	IaaS	Infrastructure as a Service
BSA	Business Software Alliance	ICS	industrial control systems
BYOD	bring your own device	ICS-CERT	Industrial Control Systems – Cyber Emergency Response Team
CAB	change advisory board	IEC	International Electrotechnical Commission
CAL	client access licence	ISA	International Society of Automation
CEO	chief executive officer	ISO	International Organization for Standardization, commonly understood as International Standards Organization
CFF	critical failure factor		
CFO	chief financial officer		
CI	configuration item	ITAM	IT asset management
CIO	chief information officer	ITAMaaS	ITAM as a Service
CIS	Center for Internet Security	ITAMS	IT asset management system
CMDB	configuration management database	ITIL	A trademarked name for a set of practices for service management, originally developed by the UK government. Originally it was an acronym for the IT Infrastructure Library.
CMS	configuration management system		
CMU	customer-managed usage		
COA	certificate of authenticity		
COTS	commercial off-the-shelf software		
CPE	common platform enumeration	ITSM	IT service management
CSC	critical security controls	JSON	JavaScript Object Notation
CSF	critical success factor	KPI	key performance indicator
DCiM	data centre infrastructure management	MAC	media access control, as in 'MAC address', used for network addressing
DML	definitive media library		
Ent	entitlement schema	MDM	mobile device management
EULA	end-user licence agreement	MSS	management system standard
HAM	hardware asset management	NIST	National Institute of Standards and Technology
		NVD	National Vulnerability Database

OEM	original equipment manufacturer	SANS	SANS Institute (SysAdmin, Audit, Network and Security)
OT	operational technology	SCAP	Security Content Automation Protocol
PaaS	Platform as a Service	SHC	supported hardware catalogue
PMU	publisher-managed usage	SKMS	service knowledge management system
RACI	responsible, accountable, consulted, informed	SLA	service level agreement
ROI	return on investment	SLM	service level management
RUM	resource utilization measurement	SSC	supported software catalogue
SaaS	Software as a Service	SWID tag	software identification tag
SACM	service asset and configuration management	TCO	total cost of ownership
		VSF	variable success factor
SAM	software asset management	XML	extensible mark-up language
SAMaaS	SAM as a Service	XSD	XML schema definition

Glossary

asset

The term 'asset' is generally used to refer to any resource or capability. The assets of a service provider include anything that could contribute to the delivery of a service. Within this guide, however, it is used to refer to hardware, software, services and the IT asset management system itself. It does not include people, documents, films, recordings and data such as contact databases.

bring your own device (BYOD)

The practice of allowing employees of an organization to use their own computers, smartphones or other devices for work purposes and access corporate information and systems.

Business Software Alliance (BSA)

Established in 1988, BSA is a trade group representing a number of the world's largest software publishers. Its principal activity is trying to stop copyright infringement. It is also referred to as the Software Alliance.

Center for Internet Security (CIS)

A not-for-profit organization founded in 2000, whose mission is to 'enhance the cyber security readiness and response of public and private sector entities, with a commitment to excellence through collaboration'.

certificate of authenticity (COA)

A seal or small sticker provided with computer software. Software COAs generally have a licence number on them and security features which verify that the software is genuine.

certification

Issuing a certificate to confirm an organization's compliance with a standard. Certification includes a formal audit by an independent body. The term is also used to mean awarding a certificate to provide evidence that a person has achieved a qualification.

client access licence (CAL)

A commercial software licence allowing clients to connect to server software and use their services.

commercial off-the-shelf (COTS)

Pre-existing software that can be purchased commercially. It is a term used to describe the purchase of products that are standard and manufactured rather than customized or bespoke.

common platform enumeration (CPE)

A structured naming scheme for IT systems, software and packages. It includes a formal naming format, a method for checking names against a system, and a description format for binding text to names within a central CPE dictionary.

configuration management

See service asset and configuration management.

configuration management database (CMDB)

A database used to store configuration records throughout their lifecycle. The configuration management system maintains one or more configuration management databases, and each database stores attributes of configuration items, and relationships with other configuration items.

configuration management system (CMS)

A set of tools, data and information that is used to support service asset and configuration management. The CMS is part of an overall service knowledge management system and includes tools for collecting, storing, managing, updating, analysing and presenting data about all configuration items and their relationships. The CMS may also include information about incidents, problems, known errors, changes and releases. The CMS is maintained by service asset and configuration management and is used by all ITSM processes. *See also* configuration management database.

configuration record

A record containing the details of a configuration item. Each configuration record documents the lifecycle of a single configuration item. Configuration records are stored in a configuration management database and maintained as part of a configuration management system.

counterfeit software

Non-genuine software that appears to be genuine, including its related proof-of-licence materials. It typically includes code from genuine software, but has modifications (e.g. to bypass licensing restrictions and/or add malware).

critical security controls (CSC)

A prioritized list of the 20 most important security controls that help in the prevention of security breaches, produced by the SANS organization. It is now maintained by the Center for Internet Security, and is also referred to as the 'CIS controls'.

critical success factor (CSF)

Something that must happen if an IT service, process, plan, project or other activity is to succeed.

customer-managed usage (CMU)

Refers to the situation where the responsibility for software licence management lies with the customer/end-user organization.

definitive media library (DML)

One or more locations in which the definitive and authorized versions of all software configuration items are securely stored. The definitive media library may also contain associated configuration items such as licences and documentation. It is a single logical storage area even if there are multiple locations. The definitive media library is controlled by service asset and configuration management and is recorded in the configuration management system.

effective licence

The right to use a specific full product (e.g. software), with its associated terms and conditions, separate from the formal licence(s). Potentially it consolidates the use rights, terms and conditions of multiple underlying licences. It is not transactional, but represents information consolidated from one or more licensing transactions. It may change over time (e.g. depending on the latest product which has been released if an underlying licence gives upgrade rights). *See also* licence; entitlement.

end-user licence agreement (EULA)

A legal contract between a software publisher or vendor and the user of the software establishing the purchaser's right to use the software. It specifies in detail the rights and restrictions that apply to the use of the software.

enterprise licence agreement

An agreement to license all employees (and contractors) within an organization accessing a software or service, normally for a specified period of time and cost.

entitlement

The right to use a specific product (e.g. a specific software product), with its associated terms and conditions, separate from the formal licence(s). This term may be used in two different senses:

■ The use rights, terms and conditions associated with a specific licence
■ The use rights, terms and conditions associated with a combination of licences (i.e. an effective licence).

'Entitlement' is more generally understood in the second sense (i.e. as a synonym for effective licence). *See also* licence; effective licence.

entitlement schema (Ent)

The encoding of software entitlements and related licensing terms and conditions. It is intended to be supplied at the time a licence is obtained, typically via a totally different route from that of the software itself. For more information refer to ISO/IEC 19770-3.

extensible mark-up language (XML)

A language that defines a set of rules for encoding documents in a format that is readable by humans and machines. XML is a flexible way to create information formats and share structured data electronically.

freeware

Software that is available free of charge, for the use of which a licence is generally required.

function

A team or group of people and the tools or other resources they use to carry out one or more processes or activities – for example, the service desk. The term also has two other meanings:

■ An intended purpose of a configuration item, person, team, process or IT service. For example, one function of an email service may be to store and forward outgoing mails, while the function of a business process may be to despatch goods to customers.
■ To perform the intended purpose correctly, as in 'The computer is functioning.'

functional management processes for IT assets

The processes in SAM/ITAM that apply across the IT asset lifecycle and deal with specific issues related to IT assets (e.g. change management, licence management and security).

hardware asset management (HAM)

All the infrastructure and processes necessary for the effective management, control and protection of the IT hardware assets within an organization, throughout all stages of their lifecycles.

Industrial Control Systems – Cyber Emergency Response Team (ICS-CERT)

An organization that works to reduce risks within and between all critical infrastructure sectors by partnering with law enforcement agencies and the intelligence community, coordinating efforts across government agencies and their control systems.

International Society of Automation (ISA)

A not-for-profit technical society for engineers, technicians, business people, educators and students who work, study or are interested in industrial automation and the activities related to it, such as instrumentation.

ISO 9001

An international standard for quality management systems.

ISO/IEC 19770

A generic term that refers to a number of international standards and guidelines for IT asset management systems. See www.iso.org for more information.

ISO/IEC 19770-1

ISO specification for an IT asset management system.

ISO/IEC 20000

A generic term that refers to a number of international standards and guidelines for ITSM systems. See www.iso.org for more information.

ISO/IEC 20000-1

ISO specification for an ITSM system. ISO/IEC 20000 is aligned with ITIL best practice.

ISO/IEC 27000

A generic term that refers to a number of international standards and guidelines for information security management systems. See www.iso.org for more information.

ISO/IEC 27001

An international specification for information security management.

ISO/IEC 55001

ISO specification for a general asset management system.

IT asset management (ITAM)

All the infrastructure and processes necessary for the effective management, control and protection of the IT assets within an organization, throughout all stages of their lifecycles.

IT asset management system (ITAMS)

The management system responsible for the effective management, control and protection of all IT assets within an organization, throughout all stages of their lifecycles.

IT infrastructure

All of the hardware, software, networks, facilities, etc. that are required to develop, test, deliver, monitor, control or support applications and IT services. The term includes all of the information technology but not the associated people, processes and documentation.

ITIL®

A set of best-practice publications for ITSM. Owned by AXELOS, ITIL gives guidance on the provision of quality IT services and the processes, functions and other capabilities needed to support them. The ITIL framework is based on a service lifecycle and consists of five lifecycle stages (service strategy, service design, service transition, service operation and continual service improvement), each of which has its own supporting publication. There is also a set of complementary ITIL publications providing guidance specific to industry sectors, organization types, operating models and technology architectures. See https://www.axelos.com/itil for more information.

key performance indicator (KPI)

A metric that is used to help manage an IT service, process, plan, project or other activity. Many metrics may be measured, but only the most important of these are defined as key performance indicators and used to actively manage and report on the process, IT service or activity.

licence

The formally documented right to use something (e.g. software), with its associated terms and conditions. It is transactional (i.e. it is obtained at a specific time; for example, as the result of a commercial sales transaction, or as the result of some other action such as agreeing to a 'click-through' licence before downloading or running software). It may be for a full product, or it may be usable only in combination with another licence. *See also* effective licence; entitlement.

licence harvesting

The process for the recovery and reuse of software and software licences that are unused or no longer required.

lifecycle

The various stages in the life of an IT service, asset, configuration item, incident, problem, change, etc. The lifecycle defines the categories for status and the status transitions that are permitted.

lifecycle management processes for IT assets

The processes and activities required to manage IT assets throughout the stages of their lifecycles, from specification through to retirement.

management system processes for IT asset management

The generic management system areas that provide the overall guidance, control and direction for the integration of all the supporting processes and activities within the ITAMS.

metric

Something that is measured and reported to help manage a process, IT service or activity. *See also* key performance indicator.

mission

A short but complete description of the overall purpose and intentions of an organization. It states what is to be achieved, but not how this should be done. *See also* vision.

National Institute of Standards and Technology (NIST)

A measurement standards laboratory and a non-regulatory agency of the US Department of Commerce. Its mission is to promote innovation and industrial competitiveness.

National Vulnerability Database (NVD)

The US government repository of standards-based vulnerability management data, which enables automation of vulnerability management, security measurement and compliance. The NVD includes security checklists, security-related software flaws, misconfigurations, product names and associated impact metrics.

off-the-shelf

See commercial off-the-shelf.

pirated software

Legitimate software that is intentionally installed beyond what is permitted by its licensing terms and conditions. (The term 'pirate' is sometimes used to refer to all underlicensing, but more accurately it implies intent, or at least serious negligence.)

point solution

Software application that addresses a single requirement or narrow range of requirements. An example is a tool which measures usage according to a software publisher's unique metrics.

policy

Formally documented management expectations and intentions. Policies are used to direct decisions and to ensure consistent and appropriate development and implementation of processes, standards, roles, activities, IT infrastructure, etc.

publisher-managed usage (PMU)

The situation where the responsibility for software licence management lies with the software publisher.

push and pull technology

Technology for installing software on client devices. Push technology is initiated by administrators from the server side. Pull technology is initiated by the end-user from the client side.

RACI

A model used to help define roles and responsibilities. RACI stands for responsible, accountable, consulted and informed.

resource utilization measurement (RUM)

A standard logging structure for recording usage information whether it is against licence entitlements or any other type of resource. For more information refer to ISO/IEC 19770-4.

role

A set of responsibilities, activities and authorities assigned to a person or team. A role is defined in a process or function. One person or team may have multiple roles – for example, the roles of configuration manager and change manager may be carried out by a single person. Role is also used to describe the purpose of something or what it is used for.

Security Content Automation Protocol (SCAP)

A method for using specific standards to enable automated vulnerability management, measurement and policy compliance evaluation. It is used to enumerate software flaws and configuration issues related to security.

service asset and configuration management (SACM)

The process responsible for ensuring that the assets required to deliver services are properly controlled, and that accurate and reliable information about those assets is available when and where it is needed. This information includes details of how the assets have been configured and the relationships between assets. *See also* configuration management system.

service level

Measured and reported achievement against one or more service level targets. The term is sometimes used informally to mean service level target.

shadow IT

All IT that is managed directly by end-users without the involvement or knowledge of IT or procurement.

shareware

Software that is initially available free of charge, but for the continued use of which a fee is generally required.

software asset management (SAM)

All the infrastructure and processes necessary for the effective management, control and protection of the software assets within an organization, throughout all stages of their lifecycles.

SAM as a Service (SAMaaS)

Software asset management delivered as a service, which typically means delivered using the SAM service provider's remote computer resources, plus specialist skills and knowledge provided by the SAM service provider.

software identification (SWID) tag

A small file that provides metadata for the authoritative identification of software. It can also provide additional authoritative metadata for the management of that software, including security automation.

stakeholder

A person who has an interest in an organization, project, IT service, etc. Stakeholders may be interested in activities, targets, resources or deliverables. Stakeholders may include customers, partners, employees, shareholders, owners, publishers, etc. *See also* RACI.

supported hardware catalogue (SHC)

A catalogue of agreed, preferred hardware products and suppliers.

supported software catalogue (SSC)

A catalogue of agreed, preferred software products and suppliers.

true-up

A provision in a software licence agreement whereby additional licences are purchased only periodically (e.g. yearly) to cover all additional usage since the last time.

vision

A description of what the organization intends to become in the future. A vision is created by senior management and is used to help influence culture and strategic planning. *See also* mission.

volume-licensing agreement

A method of licensing used by software publishers to allow organizations that need multiple product licences, but do not need multiple copies of the software media and documentation. It typically offers organizations lower pricing and the rights to copy the software onto multiple devices.

XML schema definition (XSD)

A specification for the elements in an XML document. XSD can be used to express a set of rules, with which an XML document must conform in order to be considered valid.

Index

Index